"FRIDAY'S HEROES makes the fight game come alive again...Willie Pep's great story should be read by everyone. I loved it."

-Jack Dempsey

"Mark up another win for Willie Pep! FRIDAY'S HEROES is required reading for every fight fan...And for the non-fight fan, this book is a lesson in humanity."

-Budd Schulberg

"These men who fought in the ring who I saw on T.V. in the 1950's are no longer strangers to me. They are men with ambition and hope like most other men I ever met. What I owe Willie Pep and Robert Sacchi for this introduction is a debt of gratitude. Thanks Willie and Bob,"

-Earl Wilson

This book is being re-issued as it was originally published in 1974.

Willie Pep In Stance As World Featherweight Champion 1942-1951

WILLIE PEP REMEMBERS...

FRIDAY'S HEROES

With
Robert Sacchi

Paperback version produced by James Russo

Bloomington, IN Milton Keynes, UK

author**HOUSE**®

AuthorHouse™
1663 Liberty Drive, Suite 200
Bloomington, IN 47403
www.authorhouse.com
Phone: 1-800-839-8640

AuthorHouse™ UK Ltd.
500 Avebury Boulevard
Central Milton Keynes, MK9 2BE
www.authorhouse.co.uk
Phone: 08001974150

Paperback version published by AuthorHouse 2/8/2008

ISBN: 978-1-4343-0183-3 (e)
ISBN: 978-1-4343-0182-6 (sc)

Printed in the United States of America
Bloomington, Indiana

This book is printed on acid-free paper.

Foreword by Joey Adams

Book sleeve designed by: galleryWORKS / Ryan Brookhart

Photo Preparation by: galleryWORKS / Ryan Brookhart

Special Materials Coordinated by David Wilson

Fighters on cover: Rocky Marciano and Ezzard Charles

Friday's Heroes, Inc.
New York, New York

DEDICATION:

To anyone who has stepped inside the Ring

TABLE OF CONTENTS

FOREWORD

I LOVED WILLIE PEP REMEMBERS: "FRIDAY'S HEROES". Anybody that steps into the ring is a hero to me - any night of the week. There are no cowards in the fight game. Even the losers have to face a Joe Louis or a Rocky Marciano, a Jack Dempsey or a Sugar Ray Robinson, a Tony Canzoneri or a Willie Pep. You've got to have plenty of guts to get in there with those kind of killers- and Willie Pep was one of the greatest heroes of them all. He kept on fighting even when his resources were gone and yet still maintained the dignity of a true champion.

Now, take the case of one of the greats of all time- Tony Canzoneri. He made millions in the ring and was five times World Champion, but was broke and he was joining my show. It was his debut as a performer and we were getting $50 for four days to break in our act. After three weeks of rehearsing, Tony showed up five minutes before the curtain that first morning. I was furious--or as furious as you can get with a five-time Champ. "Where the hell were you" I screamed. We go on in five minutes — Aren't you nervous?" "Nervous?" he asked quietly. "Why should I be nervous? I fought a guy called Barney Ross that could knock your head off with a right or a left. There were 20,000 people at Madison Square Garden who paid to come to see me and millions more listening in—I got $250,000 for the fight and I wasn't nervous. Here I'm getting a dollar and a quarter a show, there are eleven people in the audience and I can lick everyone of them—including the ushers—So what the hell do you want me to be nervous about?'

Don't misunderstand, nobody enjoys taking a beating. I once asked Sugar Ray Robinson, "What do you like least about boxing?" and he answered: Getting hit."

Nobody is immune from getting hit. The big thing is to be able to take it and come back. That's why all boxers are heroes to me. I love the story of the fighter that was catching everything but wouldn't let them throw in the towel. "How am I doing?' He asked his second after a disastrous Eighth Round. "Pretty good," he answered as he tried to fix him up, "but as it stands now, you'll have to knock him out to get a draw."

Maxie Baer once bragged to Slapsie Maxie Rosenbloom that "Joe Louis sure knew he was in a fight – for a while there I gave him a terrific scare."

"You sure did, "Slapsie said, "he thought he killed you."

There are no cowards in boxing. Also, there are no atheists in the ring. Muhammad Ali credits his last defeat when his jaw was broken with "Not being prayed up." He claims he was spiritually unfit and had been sinning. He meant it, too, and says he learned a lot.

That doesn't mean you can make it the easy way – just by praying. You've got to be ready if you want to survive. There's the story of the Priest and the Rabbi that were watching the fight at ringside when one of the fighters got on his knees and crossed himself. "Will that help?" The Rabbi asked. "If he can punch it will, the Priest answered.

Every one of the "Champs" that Willie writes about in his book "FRIDAY'S HEROES" are my heroes every day of the week, from Rocky to Sugar Ray to Jack Dempsey to Tony Canzoneri to my friend Willie Pep-and they all believed. I keep thinking of Joe Louis' greatest one liner since the Ten Commandments. It was a big war benefit during World War II at Madison Square Garden and the Champ was asked to say a few words to give us all a little hope. Joe said simply: "We can't lose – God is on our side."

Joey Adams
May 1973

PROLOGUE

"A QUICK FLASHBACK"

Autumn Wine

ATTENDING THE VERY EARLY GREEK THEATER must have been a great deal like watching Willie Pep fight. Those who claim to say that in the days before the Aeschylus, the plot was always the same and audiences came only to see how well the players performed their roles. Probably there are critics who would argue that theater hasn't changed. At any rate, Willie hasn't. His drink is autumn wine now, but when you watch his televised shadow flitting across the screen you know that time cannot wither nor custom stale the little desperado's incomparable gifts… Willie was *Manolete* and Michaelangelo in the handy pocket-sized package. He is an endless delight and an unfailing surprise, and the longer he goes the more astonishing he becomes.…

We hadn't been in the new house a week when Chico called to remind me of Friday's benefit down in Pennsylvania. It wasn't the best timing, what with all the confusion of moving into the new house, and Christmas just around the corner. But, I like to do these things, and for Chico Vejar I couldn't say no.

For Chico, whose son died of Cerebral Palsy, it's been his life for a long time, organizing benefits to help other kids. He wants to help everybody who's got a problem and he would, too, if it were possible. But he does what he can, like Friday for instance. It would be Christmas Eve making something very special for some kids in Appalachia. Yes, that's Chico, a man with a useful life, and he's happy.

Besides, a lot of the guys would be there and we'd have a good time seeing each other again, talking about the good old days and what we're doing now. Chico Vejar is an example of the kind of generosity you find among fighters. They are always trying to help people, themselves, and particularly kids. It seems they are always attending a benefit like this one down in Appalachia for the crippled kids in the hospital. Fighters never have their hands out like some of the other athletes in other sports; they're class guys, all the way.

So here I was all tickled pink with the new house. (We're going to paint it green in the spring.) Anyway, Ma was over, my wife Gerri's parents, and some friends had dropped by. The puppy, Huki, was stealing my daughter Melissa's cake and she was three, and crying. I had just finished shoveling the driveway and I was dying to relax, maybe take a nap, yet I had to find some things and get ready to leave in the morning. Everyone was moving.

So I went down to our finished basement to look for some publicity photos of me in the pile of boxes my wife had stacked full of my trophies and fight gear. There I found my father-in-law looking through one of my old scrapbooks. It's a funny thing. My father-in-law is Nat Volpe, who was an all-American basketball player at Manhattan College back in 1936-37 and now he coaches the game at the University of Scranton. He's a sports nut, but somehow the two of us never got around to talking about boxing much. Well, that scrapbook got us going and we sat around and talked about some of my old fights and my career for over an hour.

I was around for a long time, and retired in 1959 after twenty-one years in the ring, though that didn't stick. I came back later for a time. I was a champ, featherweight champion of the world, for nine years. I fought them all and I had a good career. You know, I made over a million bucks fighting. Of course, we didn't have very good money managers in those days, but times have changed. Today a guy like Ali gets two and a half million for one fight. One fight! And that kid Buchanan got $150,000 to fight Rocky (Roberto) Duran just a while ago. But I've got no complaints. I got $92,000 when I defended against Saddler, and that was hard work. Saddler was "one hell" of a fighter.

Like I said, boxing was good to me, very good. Where else would someone like me have gotten that kind of dough? I took care of myself and I lasted a long time. I had sixty-two amateur fights and I lost only three of them. Then I turned pro and won sixty-two in a row, winning the title in the fifty-sixth. I was the first guy to win a title undefeated. Later on I had a streak of seventy-three in a row. Those are the two longest undefeated streaks in the history of the game. I went on to have 241 pro fights, losing only 11 of them. That's a career I'm proud of, but it's funny how fast they forget. But I've got no complaints – no money, but no complaints. You can't live in the past; you've got to look to the future, and as long as people around me are happy, I'm okay.

The next morning I packed my things, had a quick late breakfast and I was on my way. The plan was to pick up some of the guys in town and meet Chico and the others at Newark Airport. Now Wethersfield, Connecticut, is just a stone's throw from Hartford, where I grew up. I rolled my blue caddy slowly through town, especially with the roads being a little slick, yet nobody paid any special attention to my WPEP license plate. People are nice, but like I said, they forget – even little reminders.

I took a little detour past the big white house I bought my mom and dad when I was champion. And that house always brought back memories. It was a long way up from my beginnings. My parents were from the other side, as we Italians say. My old man was from Syracuse in Sicily and couldn't read or write in English. He was a construction worker and things were pretty tough during the depression.

I started fighting amateur back in 1937-1938. I was fifteen and a half years old, and I got eight or nine dollars for a fight. After the fight I'd run home to my mother and give her the money. Later my father would come into the room and give me a buck. Well, naturally, that didn't go too good with me.

One night up at Crystal Lake I boxed twice and at the end of the night I had fifty dollars. I also had my eye on a sports jacket and a pair of pants that cost ten dollars, but I knew that if I took the fifty dollars home, my father would give me only a couple of bucks. So I took ten dollars and hid it. I went home that night with forty dollars, and Ma said, "Willie where did you get this money?" I told her I made it boxing. At that time my father was working at the WPA for fifteen dollars a week. When my dad came home Ma said, "Willie brought home forty dollars. Maybe he did somethin' wrong?" You know, after all, they didn't really know, and I'd been gone all day. So my father took me into the other room, closed the door and said, "Where did you get this money? You can tell me. You know your mother." I said, "Dad, I boxed tonight. I boxed tonight and got forty dollars." All this time the ten dollars was almost burning in my shoe. He said he thought forty bucks was good money for boxing and then he reached over and gave me two dollars. Then he said, if you fought tonight and you got forty dollars see if you can fight twice a week from now on." My old man, he was a sports fan.

That's how I got my start. The guy, who was fooling around, training me at the time, said to my pop, "Willie, he's a pretty good fighter. Be sure he gets to bed every night before eleven and be sure he does his roadwork every morning." So my dad became like a part-time trainer. For example, I might be out on the corner talking with someone and he'd come out and say, "Willie, go home. You gotta fight next Tuesday." And I'd say it was only nine-thirty. But he could only say, "No Willie, go home. So I'd go. Next morning he'd wake me up at six o'clock and say, "Willie, you gotta do your roadwork, you gotta fight next Tuesday." So I'd get up. Then, naturally since I was up I figured I might as well do the roadwork. Of course pop, he'd go back to bed, naturally, because it was only six o'clock. He was a big sports fan, my pop.

Pretty soon I was heading up out of town toward the Merrit Parkway. I don't use the new thruway. Like I said, I don't drive fast and I'd rather take the old roads I used to take. Soon I passed the Dunkin' Donut shop they put up a couple of years ago. I laugh to myself every time I pass it. Since I was a kid I've had a passion for donuts. When I was about fifteen years old, boxing amateur, I had a manager that, well, he was really tough on the buck. He didn't spend money too freely.

For example, on the day of my fight he would bring me in a restaurant and say, "Willie, what do you want for breakfast?" Well, I was just fifteen and I was used to crackers and milk at home, so all I could think to say was, Could I have a donut and coffee?"

As he patted me on the back, he'd say, "Willie, that's what some of the best fighters in the world train on." To the counterman he'd say, "Give this kid two donuts and a cup of coffee."

Now it's still the day of the fight and when we came back for the meal which was supposed to be a steak – at that time a pretty nice steak dinner would cost about $1.75 – he asked me what I wanted and I said, "Well, gee Buster, I'd like some scrambled eggs." "Give this kid *three* scrambled eggs," he told the waitress, without a smile. He didn't care. Though there were a few people like Buster in the fight business there were also a lot of nice ones. I guess Buster was just Buster.

We used to fight out of Norwich, Connecticut, sometimes at this place called DU-WELL A.C. I always got a kick out of that. The DU-WELL A.C. I was amateur flyweight champion of Connecticut at the time and we used to fight the Salem-Crescent A.C. from Harlem, New York. Black kids who could really fight. Anyway, I saw this real tall kid come in and when I said to my manager, "Who's that?" he said, "That's the guy you're gonna fight." I said, "Be serious, look at that guy." You see, at the time, I was a flyweight. I weighed about 105 pounds, and this guy was about 128, a featherweight. So Buster said, "Don't worry, don't worry. He can't be any good fighting you." Well I fight this guy and he's all over me. He's too good. Too big. He's punching me and punching me and I'm just trying to hang in there. When it ended and the guy won I heard his name was Ray Roberts. Later on I find out that, too, is a phony name because he was really Sugar Ray Robinson and he was also the Golden Gloves Featherweight Champion. Since, Ray, who fought his amateur career under his real name, Walker Smith, was amateur, he couldn't pick up any money in New York, and so he came to Connecticut where amateurs were allowed to fight for money. This was in 1938. I had changed my name at that time myself from Gugliemo (William)) Papaleo to Willie Pep. Pop, he didn't like the idea but I felt I needed a fighting name. Anyway, I got eight Dollars for that fight and my manager took seven. One thing about Buster, he was consistent.

Yes, that was my manager but you would think I would learn, even if I was just a kid. Later on he had me fighting another 128 pounder named Angelo Rodano. Now Angelo was a great amateur fighter who could take a lot of your professional featherweights today. I had won twenty straight at the time and I didn't want to lose. Buster said, "Willie, don't worry. It's more like an exhibition. You just go out and hit him". So I went out there in the first round and I hit him and knocked him down. "When he got up you could see he was mad. He swarmed all over me. I think he knocked me down 4 times in the 1st round, three times in the 2nd round, and twice in the third. I was getting stronger, but not fast enough, unfortunately. Rodano took it in four. He got crippled during World War II and that ended his career. But he would have been a great pro and a great crowd pleaser when television arrived and brought so many fighters out of the clubs and before the public.

7

As I drove closer to New York, I thought about the early days of my pro career. I began by parting ways with my "donut manager" Buster and getting the manager and the trainer I had throughout my career. My trainer was Bill Gore, the man who trained the Light-Heavyweight Champion of the - World, Emilio Bettina, and he was a great trainer for me. Most recently, Bill trained Cleveland Williams, Roy Harris and Manny Gonzales when he fought Emile Griffith for the Welterweight title. Bill is now eighty-four years old and is in Florida. What I owe this man can't be expressed in words, except it's a great deal. My manager was Lou Viscusi out of Florida and he managed me up to my retirement in 1959. What a change in the money. When I was boxing for Lou it was 50-50, though that's not how it began. (When I came back, George Shepard, he was my agent, would take only 10 percent, a big drop from 50.) The contract read that I would get two-thirds and Lou would get one third. Expenses would come off of the top. But there was some small lettering that if I ever got to be champion it would go to 50-50. Being champion seemed somewhat far away then. But I was fortunate and two and a half years later I was champion. So it wasn't coffee and donuts. He was a good manager and he treated me fairly.

It was awful tough at the beginning. I was seventeen and a half, a four round fighter, and not getting much work around New York. So two fellas and myself jumped into a car and drove to California from Connecticut. We went Route 66. When we got to California we were all broke and very, very hungry. I had my boxing stuff with me, so I went up to the Main Street gym in Los Angeles, which isn't there anymore, and told this fella that I was a fighter. I wanted to fight. He said, "Okay kid, I'll be your manager. You got any money?" Since I was broke he said, "Okay, you can get a dollar a round if you spar with that guy over there." A dollar a round seemed fine at the time.

The guy's name was Manuel Ortiz, a good fighter, being he was the bantamweight champion at the time. I boxed him three rounds a day for about a week, and that three dollars a day was our feed bill. Because of this they got a four-round fight for me in the Hollywood Legion Stadium, where I got to meet George Raft, my idol at the time, who was sitting at ringside. I won my fight, too, but the funny story was I got officially fifty dollars for the fight. But my manager said, "Listen, it's five dollars for the license, five dollars for the gym use, five dollars for this and that..." In the end he handed me fifteen dollars and said,

"This is your end, Kid." Now I had already priced the bus fare – we had sold the car- and I knew we were short. So I borrowed five dollars from him against my next fight, and the next day we got on the bus and came home. That was his end.

I came back home, I trained, and a couple of years later I fought for the title and won. Then I fought Manuel Ortiz. In some pre-fight publicity his manager had said, "I remember him very well. We paid him a dollar a round in California and he isn't worth much more than that. We won't have any trouble with him". Well, I won seven out of ten rounds and $20,000. Manny passed away about three years ago. He was a good man.

The city loomed up in front of me before I knew it and I headed south on the West Side Highway to make a pickup at Jack Dempsey's. I would be picking up Steve Belloise, who is always ready to help out at benefits. Jack Dempsey's is right in the strip, the Broadway and 8th Avenue area around old Madison Square Garden. Stillman's gym used to be there, with all the promoters and fight managers hanging around. We called it "Jacobs' Beach," after fight promoter Mike Jacobs. This place was especially alive through the late forties and early fifties when the really good fighters, the cream of the crop, got a chance to fight on television. And there seemed to be dozens of good, good tough fighters in those days. Of course the small clubs suffered, too. Maybe that's why you have fewer good fighters today, that and the fact that it's easier for a kid to make a living now. Anyway television took to boxing and boxing took to TV. Now that was the real good marriage.

I would like to feel that, in a way, I had something to do with it at the beginning. I was fortunate enough to be a pro just two and a half years when I got a shot at the featherweight crown and won it. I won it from Chalky Wright, who was a great champion. That was in Madison Square Garden on November 20, 1942. I boxed him again on September 29, 1944, in the Garden and defended my title successfully. It was the first time ever a fight was televised from Madison Square Garden and it started the long series of Friday Night Fights that ended around 1964. Chalky and I each got $400 for the television rights that night (Chalky, who I had beaten for the third time in 1945, accidentally drowned in a bathtub in 1957). TV fights started when Mike Jacobs, the Garden promoter, made a contract with the Gillette Safety Razor people for them to sponsor the Friday Night Fights from the Garden.

Of course, nobody had a television set in 1944, and then World War II came around. It wasn't until 1948 - 49 that the television fights really started to boom. I guess the fights along with Uncle Miltie – Milton Berle – really sold television sets during this period. But once everybody had a television set, the television stations began losing their interest in boxing and started programming other things. But boxing sold many of the first TV sets and so I think the television and fight business owes a good deal to those guys who did the fighting.

In the forties and the fifties we all got a standard rate of $4000 for the television rights, except for the big fights, like me and Saddler. In that case we got about $15,000. Of course, by today's standards it's not that impressive. Today with the closed circuit television fights a man can make quite a bit of money. Take the Ali - Frazier title fight a couple of years ago. They both made well over 5 million. But in the forties and fifties TV fights were "free," "home TV".

Then we had a guy named Tiger Jones who used to fight almost every Friday night it seemed like. He was a crowd pleaser, what we call a trial horse. I don't mean he wasn't a good fighter; if you were a little out of shape he'd trounce you. And there were a lot of other guys who were always on TV. Chico Vejar was one. He was a good classy fighter. And then Kid Gavilan, a great champ. The "kid" was perfect for television because with him every round was exciting. He was what we call a clock watcher. He wouldn't do that much until he had about forty-five seconds in the round. Then he would explode. It would catch not just the fans' eyes but also the judges' eyes, too.

Of course, some guys got rushed because of television, meaning after four or five fights they were already getting a TV fight. I think Chuck Davey was rushed. Chuck, popular with the home viewers, got rushed into a fight with Kid Gavilan. The "Kid" was the first really good fighter Davey had fought and Gavilan destroyed him.

But that's the way it goes sometimes. Television helped a lot of guys but then it ruined the source of new fighters – the small clubs where the kids are developed. I think maybe TV will do the same to baseball someday.

As I drove along, I thought about the guys and the magic of television. In those days, when I wasn't fighting myself, I was sitting somewhere watching those Friday Night Fights. A lot of those guys would be at the benefit and others wouldn't. But they were all worth remembering, like heroes' maybe, or Friday Night television.

> *…if Willie had chosen a life of crime he could have been the most accomplished pickpocket since the Artful Dodger. He may be the only man that ever lived who could lift a sucker's poke while wearing eight-ounce gloves. In action he's a marvel. And in the record books he's a down right hoax.*
>
> *It is accepted as a fact of life in the ring that the little fellows don't last long. Many of them start young and are burned out by the time they're 25. Willie had been fighting as an amateur and professional, six years or more when he won the featherweight title from Chalky Wright, and that was away back in 1942.*
>
> *Sammy Angott was the lightweight champion then, Red Cochrane had the welterweight title frozen, Tony Zale was succeeding to the spot left vacant by Billy Soose among the middleweights, Gus Lesnevich and Joe Louis bossed the big fellows. Where were they this year, 13 years later, when Willie was fighting once a month and winning 'em all?*

Red Smith – Chicago Sun Times – 1955

"Sandy and Me"

Sandy Saddler was one of those heroes, although a lot of people thought he was a villain. But I say Sandy was all right. However, I can't really talk about Sandy right now without talking about myself just a little more.

When I was still on the West Side Highway nearing the George Washington Bridge, I saw the signs to Newark Airport and that always makes me shudder. In 1947, I was on a non-scheduled airline, a two-motor job that overshot Newark Airport and came down in the woods in Middleville, New Jersey. Five guys were killed and I lay in a New Jersey hospital for five days. I said, "Doc, my back is killing me." He said, "We can't find nothin' wrong." So I laid there. Finally I was taken to a hospital near home in Hartford and they discovered it. My fifth and sixth vertebrae in my back were broken and my leg was broken. I was there for another five days, on my back. If it had gone undetected much longer it would have healed wrong and I would have been a hunchback. It was my youth and my luck that got me over it.

I had a cast on my chest and a cast on my leg for five months, so now I told the doctor, I said, "Doc, the cast is going to come off in June." I said, "When am I going to start fighting again?"

He said, Willie, this fall, September or October, you start taking long walks around the park and then the beginning of next year we'll worry about going into the gym."

Well, I couldn't wait that long. The cast came off in June and I ran into the gymnasium. I had a fight in July. And I defended my title in September of that year, against Jock Leslie in Flint, Michigan. The doctors couldn't believe it, the fact that I was fighting and winning, I guess.

I had taken my casts off in June- the cast around my chest and the cast around my leg. I went to the gym and started loosening up. Then I started running in the park and I started training. I told my manager I wanted a fight as soon as possible. He wanted to test me and five weeks later I had a fight. I'll never forget it, with a tough little Puerto Rican kid. Victor Flores, his name was. I went ten tough rounds. Now this was *really* a test because usually you get a guy you can easily handle, but this guy was there punching at me for ten tough rounds. There were two doctors at ringside and they were totally surprised. Those ten rounds with a tough Puerto Rican kid got me back on my way.

I boxed a few more times and that September, as I said, I defended my title against Jock Leslie, who was the number one contender, in his home town. Now when you go into a home town you've got to beat your man without a doubt or you won't get it, and this was for the Championship of the World. There was no problem as to who won the fight; I stopped him in eleven rounds. My loss was that the insurance company that I was suing, they said I was better than ever, so I didn't get any money from the plane crash. I think I got $15,000 for my expenses and after I paid everybody I was left with about $3000. I had sued for $250,000 but after I started boxing and winning the suit was thrown out. But I had my trunks.

One year later, in 1948, I fought Sandy Saddler for the first time. Now it's funny the way things happen. There's a story about me and Sandy that not too many people know. See, my manager, Lou Viscusi, had been friendly with the Johnston brothers for years. There was Jimmy, one of the best managers around, and Ned, who handled Jimmy's fighters, and Charley, who learned from Jimmy and became a great manager himself. And finally there was Bill, who started out managing boxers but later switched to wrestling. Anyway, Bill came to Lou one day and said he had a kid who he'd like to get started and

 13

couldn't we put him in a four rounder. So Lou says okay and the kid comes up. He's a tall skinny Negro kid and he wins his fight and we forget about him. A couple of weeks later Bill calls again and asks if he can't get the kid in a six. So Lou puts him in against Jock Leslie and in the third round Leslie knocks him out.

Now that's all we knew about the kid. His name was Sandy Saddler and nobody ever heard of him. We forgot about him. The next thing we know Bill Johnston has turned Sandy over to his brother Charley and Charley started to move him. He had him fight some in New York, but mostly out of state, in New Jersey and Pennsylvania, Detroit and Boston, New Orleans and Caracas, Jamaica and Havana, Aruba and Honolulu, almost any place where he could get him in.

Sandy was coming along but nobody in New York paid much attention. Then suddenly he's the number one contender. So Charley Johnston came around to Lou again and asked to get Sandy in a main event in New York to show what he could do. The arrangement was with Bobby Thompson and he wins but he doesn't look all that good. The boxing writers therefore said that Willie Pep doesn't have to lose any sleep worrying about Sandy Saddler.

However, Sandy was the number one contender so we made the match. But I wasn't even a little worried. I had just stopped Jock Leslie, who had whipped Sandy. I had won seventy-three fights in a row and I didn't think any kid named Sandy Saddler was going to beat me. So we fought. It was in Madison Square Garden on October 29, 1948. I started out feinting as usual to get a feeling for him and he ignored it completely and waded in and caught me cold. I was completely surprised. He knocked me down twice before the fourth round and then he stopped me.

We had a rematch. It was set for February 11, 1949 and you better believe I was ready for him. Most of the writers were picking Sandy, but I was ready for him. I was dead set on beating him no matter what. That night we had the fight of our lives. A lot of people who know what they're talking about rate it as one of the greatest fights, and I just happen to be very proud of that fight. As Casey Stengel would say, "You could look it up."

As I said, I was ready for him that time. I was in great condition and my timing was sharp. I was boxing as good as ever. By the eleventh round I was way ahead. I had won at least eight rounds and Sandy had to knock me out to win. Now they say Sandy was dirty but he was just rough and tough, which was the way to beat me. Besides, he had four or five inches in height on me and was as hard a puncher as anybody I ever boxed, second only to Chalky Wright, who was the hardest hitter ever in the featherweight division.

Anyway, Sandy knew what he had to do and from the twelfth on he really came at me. But I was ready and boxing my best. I was thinking and jabbing well and keeping him away with good right hands and then tying him up. I had him off balance most of the time but he was desperate now and kept swinging with those long arms of his trying to end it all with one punch. But I had him mostly off balance and only a few of his shots were real hard. He tried desperately but he couldn't put me down. I had my title back. And besides the packed Madison Square Garden, thousands and thousands throughout the country had seen it on television, way back in 1949. It was a great fight for lots of people.

We fought again in 1950 and that was a good fight, too, only rougher. It was going along close with me leading on points when all of a sudden my shoulder snapped and it hurt bad. I couldn't lift my arm and there was no way I could continue unless I wanted to fight Sandy with one hand. It was around the eighth or ninth round. I couldn't continue and Sandy was the Champ again.

We fought for the last time on September 26, 1951, in one of the roughest, toughest fights of all times, and in some ways one of the most controversial. Not that there was any doubt about who won. After all, I was cut and couldn't continue. This time my left eye was completely shut and I was fighting with one eye. I was ahead on points by the end of the eighth round but I couldn't continue, so the fight had to be his.

But there was controversy. First of all it was a real brawl, like the old time bare knuckle days, with wrestling, heeling, eye gouging, tripping, thumbing – you name it. A lot of writers thought that we should have both been thrown out. They thought Ray Miller the referee, let it get out of hand, that he should have followed his own instructions. He told us he had the power to penalize us and he wanted a clean fight. Well, I've got to admit he didn't do much. However, I'm not blaming the referee; it was me and Sandy who did it.

And that's the second point of controversy. Who was most to blame? Who started it? Now, quite a few writers said it was my fault, but that's ridiculous. I'm not saying I was blameless, but look at it this way. Sandy was the tough guy; I was the boxer. It didn't make any sense for me to rough it up with him. However, I did it eventually because he started it and I got mad. In the first thirty seconds Miller had to warn Sandy to lay off holding me around the neck and hitting me with his free hand. I didn't do anything that early in the fight. In fact, I was boxing good and won most of the early rounds. I know if I kept it up I would've beat him and become the only guy to hold the featherweight crown three times.

But that wasn't to be. I got mad and tried to out rough him, which wasn't my style. And the referee didn't do much, so we kept it up. In fact, one writer asked how come they bothered with a referee at all.

Anyway, my biggest problem was that he caught me in the second round and cut my right eyelid. I was hurt. I couldn't see and later in that round he knocked me down with a left to the body. There was no doubt about the fact that he really hit. After that round I boxed him good for a few rounds, making him miss and then countering. But I couldn't see well and sooner or later he would corner me and then the rough stuff would begin. It wouldn't end until we were both wrestling around on the canvas or the referee was actually outside the ring trying to pry us apart.

In the seventh round we were wrestling around and somehow my leg got tangled up around Sandy's and the referee rushed over to untie us. The referee wound up getting tangled himself and we being off balance accidentally caused him to fall down. It resulted in a very funny scene. The spectators roared with laughter and poor Ray Miller was red with embarrassment.

When he picked himself off the canvas, Sandy still had me tied up like a pretzel. Miller got mad and said, "Break, break you S.O.B.'s or I'll suspend both of you."

In the next round, Sandy came out and deliberately back-handed me across the face as I was on the ropes. The referee didn't say a thing. So I proceeded to jab and get behind Sandy and deliberately tripped him. Miller warned me. My fans seeing that only I was being reprimanded, charged the ring screaming at the referee for being one-sided. Charley Johnston climbed onto the ring apron and screamed at the referee for allowing me to trip Sandy. Poor Ray Miller got it from both ends.

Anyway, it went on like that and my eye got worse and worse till I couldn't see at all. You can't fight with one eye, not against Sandy Saddler, and not in a fight like that. At the start of the ninth round I couldn't continue. It was over.

We had wrestled in the fifth, sixth and seventh besides in the eighth. We were strangling each other and there was gouging and heeling throughout. In spite of, or despite, all this, Ray Miller had me ahead five rounds to three on his card. I was also ahead on the judges' scorecards. But I lost; that was my 165th fight and only my fourth loss. It was my third TKO loss, all three to Sandy. He had knocked out 89 guys in 130 fights to that time. He could certainly hit.

A funny bit about this bout was Robert Christenberry, the new boxing commissioner. At the weigh-in he passed the remark that he liked wrestling. He saw it that night. After the fight he didn't say much except that "these boys don't like each other."

Of course the boxing commission was not happy with this brawl we staged and Christenberry, making his first major decision as commissioner, suspended Sandy and me from boxing in the state of New York for an indefinite period. I can't blame him. We had broken all the rules that night.

It took quite a few months for the commission to cool off and when they did we both were reinstated. In the meantime, I had won fifteen straight outside of New York and my popularity was as strong as ever. The International Boxing Commission booked me into the first open date - a Friday Night television spot against a tough up and coming Pat Marcune. I beat Marcune bad, real bad, and once again I was in good standing with the New York Commission. Nothing succeeds like success.

Now, a lot of people think there was an antagonism between Sandy and me. Maybe there was during our fights – but we're friendly now. I've boxed him several times since in charity exhibitions and we get along fine. When we were fighting for the championship I wanted to lick him in the worst way and he wanted to lick me. Well, we went all out. But I have no hard feelings and we get along. No complaints here.

It's a funny thing about styles. I beat a lot of guys who beat Sandy. Yet he beat me three out of four times. Humberto Sierra beat Sandy and I beat Sierra twice. Paddy DeMarco beat Sandy twice and I beat

DeMarco. Strange. If you don't have the right style you're going to get licked, and if you don't fight your own fight you're going to get licked. I tried to get rough with Saddler and you usually can't beat a man at his own game. Not that man.

A year after our last bout, Sandy got drafted into the Army. This was early in 1952. The National Boxing Association thought it would be a good idea to have an 'interim champion' to help keep the interest alive in the featherweight division until Sandy got back. The "interim champion" not only would fill in for Saddler during his absence but would automatically be recognized as the number one challenger against the returning Saddler.

Percy Basset became the "interim champion' and the European boxing officials went along with this by matching Bassett with France's Ray Famechon. I had beat Ray several years earlier in a title bout. Anyway, Bassett stopped Famechon and was now the undisputed 'interim champion."

But Bassett never did get that crack at Sandy.

Instead, he was asked to meet Lulu Perez in an elimination match and the winner would positively be given a go with Saddler. Bassett stopped Perez, but neither man got a title shot.

After he was discharged in 1954, Sandy continued his tune-up bouts and still wasn't ready to defend his title. But, he said, he would consider the winner of a Bassett-"Red Top" Davis match.

So Bassett got into the elimination against Davis and he lost in twelve rounds at Madison Square Garden. Poor Percy, after all that fighting and no title bout with Saddler.

In 1955 Sandy met Davis in his first title defense since the last one he had with me in 1951 and kayoed Davis. He went on to kayo Lulu Perez and then lose a non-title decision to Joe Lopes that year.

The same year he lost a non-title bout to Flash Elorde. As a result, a title bout was set with 'Elorde in 1956 because of Flash's good showing. Sandy kayoed him.

Sandy had his last fight later on in 1956. He took a shellacking from an unranked Jewish kid called Larry Boardman in yet another non-title bout.

At age 30, Sandy had compiled an amazing record. He had a total of 162 bouts, losing 15 and a knockout ratio of almost 70 percent – 103 knockout victims, including me.

What cut Sandy's career short? Well, Sandy was involved in a crash in July, 1956. He was riding in a taxicab and struck his head against the door when the cab crashed up into the sidewalk.

He was hospitalized for about three or four weeks, and then tried to get back in shape by working out- but it didn't help.

He was constantly bothered by warnings from the boxing commission about defending his title. They finally told him to submit a medical report on his condition.

In the report, the doctor treating Saddler since the accident recommended that Sandy quit boxing if he wanted to retain his sight. And that if he continued there would be a chance of total blindness. At his age, with no "money matches" in sight and with Sandy's earning power on the downgrade, Sandy took the advice of the doctor.

It was a tough turn of events for Sandy, considering boxing was all he knew and he had worked so hard to get there.

But you know, Sandy had 160 fights and may have been experiencing some eye trouble somewhere along the way like other boxers have. Eye injuries and that threat of blindness is one of the major occupational hazards of boxers. (Sandy made a wise decision.) A lot of guys kid themselves and keep walking into the night.

But like I said, Sandy was just rough and tough and not a "dirty fighter" as people think. His almost five foot, ten inch frame, tremendous reach and the punching power of a welterweight, sometimes had the five foot, five inch opponent tangling himself to get inside on Sandy.

I have nothing but respect for Sandy. He was voted into boxing's Hall of Fame in 1971.

ROUND 2

"Ginks"

Not since the second battle of the Marne has so much French blood been shed as oozed, dripped and, at times, spouted from various wounds in the stoical face of Robert Villemain in Madison Square Garden's ring Friday night. Nor by the same token, have such large-scale American operations been noted on the French map since the Second World War, as those which Steve Belloise conducted while demonstrating to a distinctly pro-Gallic audience that those famed 50 million can be wrong in assuming all French middleweights are Cerdans just because they ape Marcel's style.

> ...Though the gore was Villemain's and he was far out classed by the Italian reincarnation of Bob Fitzsimmons... as for Belloise, he demonstrated by whipping Marcel Cerdan's gendarme that he is entitled to meet the master for the middleweight championship. Since Marcel's fame hereabouts is based on the job he did on Tony Zale, who could have been too highly rated on the strength of his bouts with Rocky Graziano, it wouldn't do to jump at the conclusion that Belloise would be fried snails for Marcel.
>
> Dan Parker – New York Daily Mirror – 1949

Instead of heading across the bridge as usual I cut down the West Side Highway to midtown to pick up Steve Belloise at Jack Dempsey's.

Ginks works towing cars for the city these days. It's a good job, a city job. You get benefits from the city. And since he got his house in the Bronx all paid for from fighting, he's doing alright.

Anyway, Ginks and I got to Jersey through the Lincoln Tunnel and we were heading for Al Certo's custom tailor shop in Secaucus to meet with some of the other guys. Now, when you come out through that tunnel it's confusing if you aren't used to it. I needed Ginks to ride shotgun.

So I asked him, "We take Route 3, don't we, Ginks?"

I had to ask him twice, Ginks, he's okay, but his mind tends to wander a lot. He's a real daydreamer. I looked at him and I could see he was probably off in Paris somewhere licking every Frenchman that would fight him.

That was his main problem in those days. He might have been remembered as one of the greatest middleweights ever. Steve Belloise. How many kids today have ever heard of him? But what a helluva puncher and a pretty good boxer, too. None of the champions of those days, Cerdan, Graziano, none of them wanted to take a chance with that one-shot counter right hand. But Steve came close, damn close, within a whisker of the middleweight crown in a day when there were great middleweights all over the place.

Steve was born in the Bronx in the Mosholu and Grand Concourse section. He was just like all the other kids up there, growing up in the Depression and hanging out on the streets; lots of time without much else to do. For one, they used to shoot craps a lot up there and Steve used to always watch a friend of his in the game. Anyway, every time that Steve would watch the game his friend would lose. Pretty soon he was calling him Jinx. Later on it was changed to Ginks and the name stuck. It's a funny thing, but the name kind of fit as it turned out.

Steve started boxing around the same time I did, a little later maybe, in 1938. One big difference, his brother Mike was a great featherweight champion from 1936-1938, and Steve was able to get on his brother's cards right away. In fact, he never fought amateur at all. He didn't really have to; he was that good.

Ginks moved right along and in 1940 he beat Ceferino Garcia, the former middleweight champion, who had just lost his title to Ken Overlin, who was real polished and loaded with style. Anyway, it gave

Ginks a crack at Overlin. Now, you've got to remember at this time Ginks was only twenty or twenty-one and didn't have much experience yet and wasn't as tough as he was going to get. But he was still tough and as game as they come. He went fifteen rounds with the slick Overlin at Madison Square Garden, not once, but twice. The referee scored both fights for Steve but the judges went the other way, maybe because Overlin was champ. Ginks had already missed twice. At that time you had one of those split title situations and Billy Soose, the NBA champ, beat Overlin later on for the world title.

Anyway, Steve joined the Navy three days after Pearl Harbor and served as an athletic instructor in the South Pacific. He went in the Navy in pretty good shape, and he got out tougher than ever. He also sort of grew up physically and those quick counters of his could take out anybody with one punch. He'd spend a whole fight watching the guy's left hand and when the guy got a little tired or careless—when that left started to drop just a wee bit after a jab- wham, Ginks' right hand cross would end it. One shot! That's all it took. Ginks could hit with the best.

I'll show you what I mean! Ginks got into Ripley's Believe It or Not once. In one of his first fights after the war he was fighting this high ranking middleweight from Portland, Maine, called Coley Welsh. Anyway, Welsh throws a jab and drops his hand and Steve counters over it with a right smack on the chin. Welsh went down and took the count of nine, got up and staggered across the ring and fell down again, took the eight count, got up again, staggered cross the ring and right back down again for the knockout.

One punch! He knocked the guy down three times with one shot! That was power. That was Ginks.

Anyway, after that he went on to trounce a lot of top-notch fighters, like Tommy Bell, Paddy Young and Georgie Abrams, who fought Tony Zale for the title and lost; and the French guy Robert Villemain, and ex-champs like Al Hostak and Anton Christoforidis and the French champ Jean Stock. By this time he was known to be dynamite and it got tougher to get the good fights.

Steve said it himself: "So what's it getting me? Does anybody hear Rocky Graziano saying I've earned a shot at his title, 'huh? Then there's that Cerdan, the great European champ. Mention my name to him, and you're talking a language he don't understand."

Of course, Steve didn't win every fight. I remember one he lost which didn't help him much with getting a title shot, but it's kind of interesting because it shows you how much interest there was in the club fights, neighborhood fights, before television. This was in 1941. It was with Tami Mauriello, who became a leading heavyweight and who also fought Joe Louis for his title in 1946. The Belloise-Mauriello fight was called the "Battle of the Bronx".

Barney Nagler of the old Bronx Home News and later the New York Post made these classic pre-fight remarks about Belloise and Mauriello.

Poor old Jonas Bronck he'll twist in his tomb this day, he'll turn over too, what with the battle of the Bronx echoing from Madison Square Garden right up to ritzy Riverdale, Poor old Jonas, what was named the Bronx after its first settler was a peaceful strip of geography. Tonight strife-torn, ripped by the Steve Belloise – Tami Mauriello 10 rounder at the Garden this very night. At long last the two Bronx middleweights, Sir Steve of Bedford and Sir Tami of Fordham, meet to establish supremacy to gain presents of about $6000 each.

Tami, a kid who learned to fight in the Golden Gloves, ended this highly ballyhoo battle in just 2:58 seconds when he scored a first round TKO over his neighbor Ginks. With a crowd of about 13,000 Tami hammered Steve to the canvas with tremendous right hands for the counts of nine, eight, and nine, and then knocked him through the ropes before the ref stopped it. Steve spotted Tami 8 pounds and that was some edge for a tough cookie like Tami. Steve got caught good and it was over quick, it was just one of those things. Tami, of course, went on to beat the best heavyweights in the forties, like Bruce Woodcock and Lee Savold. But after knocking Louis down in the first round, Joe got up and destroyed Tami.

Yeah, this was yesteryear when almost the entire country was booming with boxing clubs. Just in New York State you had about twenty clubs operating in good fight towns like Buffalo, Troy, Utica, Rochester, Syracuse, Albany and Schenectady. But by 1958-1959 most of these clubs were all closed after television killed the source of potentially good fighters. In the television era it was tough for a kid to get his ring know-how. The neighborhood clubs, once the developing grounds for young fighters, gradually disappeared from the boxing scene. Promoters were desperate for good boxers, and the managers were in a hurry for the television paydays. That was the main reason why so many kids after just a few preliminary bouts were rushed into main events before they were ready. And most of them had short careers. It's like in show business, with the young comics today. Where do they get their training? All the small nightclubs are out of business, so with little know-how these comics try a do-or-die stand on big television talk shows like Johnny Carson. If they just happen to click, they're in; if not, it's goodbye Charlie.

Ginks' big money fights were against French champion Jean Stock and Sugar Ray Robinson. In 1949 he got $15,000 to fight Stock in the Sports Palace in Paris. Ginks, with his great right hand counter, caught Stock on his chin in the sixth round and he went down for a count of nine. He got up again and Ginks hit him with a left hook and a right cross and Stock was down again. That was it for Stock. He signaled the referee, "Fini, fini."

The Ray Robinson bout of the same year was one of Ginks' last and his biggest payday, grossing him $25,000. It was the fight for the house, his house in the Bronx, that is. The fight was a ten rounder, non-title. They stopped it in the seventh round, officially, but it was in the sixth that Sugar caught Ginks on the jaw and his manager stopped the fight.

Steve's last fight was in Canada in 1951 against Laurent Dauthville. Steve lost on a technical kayo which never should have been stopped. I guess when you're in another country they'll stop anything.

Steve missed the real big ones. Graziano wouldn't fight him. Jake LaMotta, who would fight anyone no matter how big, offered him a shot, but Jake wanted almost all of the gate. That didn't go too good with Ginks, and the fight never came off.

Ginks did come close to his shot in 1949. After beating Stock, Ginks' manager, old "walkin" around Eddie Walker, " wired Ginks, who was on his way home aboard the S/S *Vulcania* that a title shot with Marcel Cerdan was set for June, 1949, at the Polo Grounds. Cerdan had beat Tony Zale for the title. By the time the boat docked Ginks was out, and replaced by Jake LaMotta who they felt was a better draw at the gate. However, if Steve had gotten a crack at Cerdan I think that we would have seen a great LaMotta-Belloise fight- that's our loss as much as Ginks'.

After retiring, Steve bounced around for a while like most of us. He spent six years tending bar and then was a bricklayer for about twelve. The last couple of years he's been towing cars for the Police Department. He doesn't tow them off the street. Just from pier to pier for storage until the owners pick them up. He's glad about that. He says he hasn't got the heart to tow them off the street. I know he means it. The image of most boxers is supposed to be mean and tough but it's not true. In the ring we all want to win and get out of there with less hurt than the other guy. That's our business. We know more than the average guy what it's like to get hurt. We develop respect for other guys. Steve doesn't care to tow cars off the street; they belong to the other guy.

It's like a job I had a few years ago. I was Tax Marshall for the state of Connecticut and I came across quite a few tough situations. You can't have a heart for a job like this and having one you get talked out of a lot of things. My job as Tax Marshall was to collect unpaid taxes from Connecticut residents. The cases I handled were the last resort. The delinquent accounts had been put through the ringer by the State Tax Department before I got to them. So I was the last resort for the state and made the final disposition. If I saw fit, I could put liens on their home, car, if they owned one, or any property they had. But doing that is kind of tough and most of the people in these cases were really broke, on their last leg. I got paid only if I collected the taxes – 6 percent of what I collected. I didn't make much money. They were the other guys.

One time I had a case in one of the towns outside of Hartford. The guy owed $3000 in taxes. I knocked on the door and his wife answered it holding a baby in her arms. She called her husband to the door and would you believe it, I knew this guy. I hadn't seen him in twenty-five years. He had bought a gas station and had taxes in arrears and now he owed $3000, which he couldn't pay. He asked me what I was doing and I told him, "I collect back taxes."

So we sat down for some coffee, with his wife holding the baby, and three others running around. He told me how tough things were since his business folded. Well, before I left, I ended up loaning this guy ninety dollars. You can't get blood out of a stone. I had the last say and this guy couldn't pay and the issue was closed for good. You can't keep going back to the people when they just don't have it. I cleared many a guy who was harassed. After six months of this I left the job. It was hard on a man.

Like most men, I like to work with what I was trained for and know best - boxing. Every now and then I get calls from the World Boxing Association to referee. I refereed five world championship matches all over the world. I do a good job for these people, but on occasion you could run into some trouble- especially abroad.

When I worked the Johnny Famechon (Ray's nephew) – "Fighting" Harada fight for the featherweight title of the world in Sydney, Australia, they had no rules for judging a fight. The promoters said to do what I thought best. I had to make up my own scorecard. So I got a piece of cardboard and ruled off the columns for fifteen rounds. They had no boxing commission. I was the sole judge.

When the fight began, I decided to use a five/four system, five points for the winner and four for the loser of the round. At the end of the fifteen rounds I added up the points and it came out even. So I called the fight a draw. Well, naturally, some liked the decision and some didn't. I then gave my scorecard to the chief of police who was sitting at ringside. In a way I should have given it to him before the decision but they had told me to give the decision as soon as the bout ended. He added up the card and said, "By Jove, Willie, you made a mistake of one point." Sure enough we re-added and we had Famechon ahead by one point. So I went back and raised Famechon's hand and that caused another turmoil. It was tough. I was referee, judge and boxing commission. In the second fight in Harada's hometown in Japan, Famechon made it unanimous by knocking him out in three rounds.

Refereeing is tough enough just keeping the fight going and protecting the fighters without being the sole judge.

As I said, Steve was into towing cars; aside from that, Belloise loved the movies. He's a real ham at heart and he's even managed to get some movie parts. He played in *Requiem for a Heavyweight* with Anthony Quinn and Jackie Gleason and he's also been in *The Godfather and the Valachi Papers* along with his buddy, Chester Rico, who lives a few blocks away from him.

Now Chester, he comes to a lot of the benefits, too, but he said he couldn't make this one. Rico was a classic lightweight boxer out of the Fordham section of the Bronx and he fought a lot of top guys in his time, but he had only one good shot at the title. He was fighting Bob Montgomery in an elimination bout and leading on all score cards when, bingo, his eye got cut. The referee stopped it in the eighth round. Montgomery went on to beat Beau Jack for the lightweight title.

He fought most of the good ones like Terry Young, Maxie Shapiro, Freddy Archer, Johnny Bratton and Tippy Larkin, the junior welterweight champ; he even fought Beau Jack twice, but not for the title. Yet, with all these names, Chester never made big money, maybe $8000 to $10,000 a year. A guy couldn't make much in those days without the big fights. For example, at the Bronx Coliseum general admission was about thirty-five or forty cents and ringside maybe a buck. Retiring in 1950, at age twenty-nine, Chester had 101 professional fights and won all but 18 of them.

Chester likes to kid Ginks about a fight he had with a Texan named "Punching Paul" Altman, Punching Paul was so mad after Steve had knocked him flat with his right that the Texan got up at the count of nine and kicked Steve full in the groin. Of course, Punching Paul was disqualified and Steve was left kind of sore. In a return match, Steve didn't give Punching Paul a chance to kick him. He knocked him cold in the first round.

During the shooting of *Requiem for a Heavyweight* Steve was asked by Mickey Rooney, one of the film's stars, what he thought about acting. Ginks said, "When a fighter turns to be an actor he has the emotions for it. I like it. In acting when the director tells you something you've got to do it. You can't hit him."

ROUND 3

"The Toughest of 'Em All"

Ginks, he had his problems, and so did a lot of guys. It's how you handle them that counts.

You may pick up a paddle, but that doesn't make you a ping pong player. But when you climb in the ring and you're a fighter, I don't care what anybody says. You climb in the ring and you accept a physical challenge. You may not be good. You may be scared to death. But you're there to fight and you're going to fight. And if you don't win on the scorecard you still win as a man. Every fighter who gets in there and gives his best knows this.

Frankie Ryff was a guy like that. I mean, he never got to be champion, but he was one heck of a fighter. How many other guys could have done what he has done?

Frankie was a handsome Irish guy, a lightweight. He, too, was from up in the Bronx. He fought as a pro from 1951-1959, which was perfect for him because he was great for television. In those days if you didn't make it on TV you couldn't make a living. The local clubs were now dead. After all, who wanted to go to a little club to watch some guys who weren't really that good when you could stay home or be in a bar and watch the best on TV?

Of course, like I said, TV was hungry for fighters with a popular image and you tended to get rushed along too fast sometimes and fight some guy you weren't ready for. A lot of times that would be the end. But if you looked good, you were a TV sweetheart and you could sit on top of the world just as a popular contender without ever fighting for the championship. And that would last until somebody new came along and knocked you off.

To digress for a moment, there was a tough Jewish kid, Larry Boardman, of New England, managed by his father, Sam, who became a new TV sweetheart when he knocked out Frankie at Madison Square Garden in 1955. It really was two big bouts in Boston earlier that year that gave Boardman the chance to show in New York's Garden and on national television for the first time.

Larry was called in as a quick substitute for the former world welterweight champ Tony DeMarco against lightweight champion Wallace "Bud" Smith at the Boston Garden. Boardman was just another kid so far as the fans were concerned. Larry was unrated before the bout. But he whipped Smith in a come-from-behind effort and was so impressive that he broke in as number ten lightweight in the world in *Ring* magazine's ratings. He followed this by giving featherweight champ Sandy Saddler one of the worst beatings of his career at the same Boston Garden. Larry then zoomed up to number seven in *Ring's* world ratings.

Boardman, after a couple of years of ups and downs, was done in by a new TV sweetheart, Johnny Busso, who kayoed him, and later Busso was done in by Carlos Ortiz and so on and so forth. And that's the way it went.

Frankie did well in the beginning and he got his shots. He beat a lot of top guys like Ralph Dupas, Paddy DeMarco, Cisco Andrade and Dennis Pat Brady, in 1954 they named him Rookie of the Year and started talking about Frankie as the future lightweight champ. That year he had pushed his winning streak to seventeen in a row by beating Orlando Zulueta, who was a good fighter.

But by then Frankie was already having his problems. Frankie cut up over the eyes too easy, and that's trouble. What made it worse was Frankie was always driving in. That was his style. He bore in. He'd take some and give some. Now, even that made him unusual because Frankie was a converted southpaw and that meant he wasn't a hard puncher. He was an exceptional boxer, but being aggressive he would keep coming and you can't duck them all.

Well, like I said about styles, you've got to fight your fight. So Frankie kept pressing, only even more to try and end the fight quick before he could get TKO'd by eye cuts. And he kept getting hit a heck of a lot around the eyes and the damage got worse and worse. But he gave a lot, too. He'd tear the house down with his fast combinations. Although Frankie continued on his winning ways, he was cutting up more and more, and eventually the referees were stopping bouts because of his torn brows.

So he finally fought Zulueta and somehow he hung in there and won the fight, but both eyes looked bad. The fight went ten rounds, ten tough rounds, and when it was over Frankie was a mess. It took thirty-four stitches to close the cuts around his eyes.

To stop the cutting, he had a three-hour operation where they parted the skin on his forehead and shaved down the bones behind his eyebrows. Supposedly, his brow bones jutted out sharply and made the skin over it very easy to cut.

Most guys would have quit, but not Frankie. Frankie is an Aries. My astrology book says that they are courageous, ambitious and forceful. Ironically, it also says that they are accident-prone. Well, he kept going. It took him months to recuperate, but he kept going. He was passionately determined to become the lightweight champ.

But from 1955 until 1959 it was all downhill for Frankie. His heart and hands were just as tough as ever, but his eyes wouldn't let him win. Finally, he got TKO'd on cuts three times in 1959 and he retired. He was an "old" man at twenty-six.

In the meantime, he had gotten married in 1955. After he retired he went to work for the Otis Elevator Company installing elevators in New York skyscrapers. But Frankie, he was a fighter at heart. He couldn't get his mind off that title, which he had dreamed about since he was a kid fighting in the Police Athletic League. So he decided to try again.

Barney Ross, the great welterweight champion in the 1930's and World War II hero, was the godfather of Frankie's daughter, Jacqueline. Barney, who also managed Frankie in 1958-59, agreed to re-manage him but only with the understanding that Frankie would quit if Whitey Bimstein, who was the trainer, said he wasn't good enough. So Frankie went into training and after just a few workouts Whitey said, "He looked so good I was amazed. He was makin' some of my stable look like novices."

So Barney and Whitey started looking for the right opponent and Frankie kept working for Otis Elevator. In January, 1962, Frankie was working on the Sperry-Rand Building on 6th Avenue, which was just going up; it was just a skeleton. He took the lift up to the eighth floor and made his way along a catwalk that led to an elevator shaft. It was a windy cold morning, particularly eight stories up, and in January the steel collects ice. Frankie's foot came down on an icy patch, and his legs flew out from under him. He slid off the catwalk and into the open shaft. He went straight down, eight and a half stories, smashing through a section of wooden planks on the second floor, which slowed him up just a little before he hit the concrete at the bottom of the shaft.

They took him to Roosevelt Hospital. An intern took one look at him and felt poor Frankie had no chance at all. But they went to work. There were so many things wrong with him that most had to be ignored while they concentrated on the one that was about to kill him any minute. The impact had fractured his skull real bad and had busted a bunch of blood vessels in his head. And all that blood and fluid was pushing hard against his brain. When they operated they were able to relieve the pressure just in time. I guess those doctors gave Frankie yet another chance and that tough Irishman took it and fought like hell against his toughest opponent.

It's ironic, but Frankie was still lying in the special care unit two months after the fall when they wheeled in Benny "Kid" Paret for emergency treatment. Frankie didn't know it though. He was still in a coma.

Anyway, you probably remember, the Kid had been knocked out by Emile Griffith in a wicked, tough title fight at Madison Square Garden and he never did regain consciousness. There was Frankie, sixty six days in a coma, breathing through a tube in his throat and being fed through his veins. And there was Benny Paret practically right alongside of him, both of them with brain damage.

Paret had taken his last and worst ring beating and Frankie the beating of his life in that elevator shaft. Benny passed away and it was a damn shame. But Frankie just wouldn't die. The doctors couldn't believe it because there was almost nothing left of him – except his heart.

Frankie's left arm was broken in a dozen places and twisted out at the elbow. His fingers were broken. His right leg was jammed up against his chest and frozen there so it couldn't be budged. His ankles were busted up and locked rigid. His body was just one big contusion and he had all kinds of internal injuries, not to mention his smashed head.

He went down from 140 pounds to about 85. His father and Mother sat by his side day after day searching for encouraging signs. Frankie finally came out of the coma five and one half months after the accident. Not knowing how he got there he soon realized that he could not talk, walk, or move his arms.

A couple of months later they moved Frankie to the Institute of Physical Medicine and Rehabilitation. His leg was still locked up tight against his chest. Painfully, inch by inch, they worked the leg down, forcing the hamstring to stretch, but it couldn't come all down all the way. Finally, they just had to operate and cut the hamstring.

Frankie was still helplessly paralyzed. He prayed that God would give him the strength to keep going and pull through. His little daughter, Jacqueline, was on his mind all the time. He just had to make it, to get out of this big sleep.

But a year after his accident Frankie got another jolt – his wife filed for divorce. Now, there are lots of reasons people get divorced, some good, some bad. Certainly, everyone likes a winner and that goes for Frankie's wife, too. But Frankie didn't look like one, speechless, all broken up in a wheelchair. You could say that the divorce wouldn't make a big difference in his life in the hospital, except for his visitors. But the big difference to Frankie at the time was going to be his daughter; he realized that he was to lose his Jacqueline. At his own expense he eventually appealed to the courts for visitation rights; his ex-wife, who remarried, felt Jacqueline should know only one father – the new one.

Divorces do something to you, especially when you're in a hospital. I never was divorced in a hospital, but I did get divorced four times. In my case, I never went looking for girls in my life; I was in the limelight, so they came to me. But being divorced four times, believe me, has its own special pains. I came from a good-sized family and all my brothers and sisters are happily married with kids; and I expected the same for me.

My first four wives cost me over a half a million dollars between settlements—fur coats, rings and the rest. They got everything they wanted. They married me for my name and my money; in the settlements I got the name and they got the money. I guess that's a successful divorce for some.

My first marriage was at age twenty. I was going out with this little girl and she said that she wanted to get married. I was nineteen at the time and successful in my professional career, making pretty good money. So I said, "Listen, I could never get married until I was champion of the world." Well, two months later, much to our surprise, I became champion of the world. So I got married, too. This was in 1942. I loved the girl but I wasn't ready for marriage. Being champion of the world and married, both at the age of twenty, was too much. It didn't take. The marriage went first, four years later. We did have two wonderful children and that's the only thing I wouldn't change. In the settlement I got custody of the children. My mother, she had just finished raising little ones of her own, started once again with my two and thanks to God it worked out well.

A boxer's life is rough. You're always on the road; you've got to be in bed before eleven and get up at six in the morning and you're not supposed to go out drinking and fooling around. It takes its toll on a wife who likes to go out and have fun. In addition, I was in the service two of the four years of my first marriage, and maybe that's where the trouble started. It certainly didn't help.

Seven months after my first divorce, I got married again. She was living in Hartford at the time and I had known her from the old neighborhood, but she was working in New York as a model and was used to some really fine clothes. Well, I was only ex-champion at the time but still a soft touch.

She had known my first wife and knew that I had bought her a mink coat. So one day she said, "Willie, it's getting cold. I think I need a coat." So I said she should go buy a coat, and she said, "A mink, of course, like you bought your other wife."

She got her mink. She wore it for two or three months and then spring came, and she then said, You know, Willie, it's awful warm wearing this coat in the spring- I'd like just a little mink cape." A cape is a half a coat, I think. Well, in any event, she got it. And when summer came I went all the way and bought her a mink stole. The marriage lasted two years and three minks. Our lives were different; we couldn't make it last.

A year or so later I met an exotic dancer; she danced so well that within several months we fell in love and got married. She was very independent and making good money dancing. But when we got married she quit her job and we stayed in my mother's apartment house in Hartford.

We had our arguments, but one day we had a big one and I stormed out of the house. I stayed out all night and got into a card game with seven other guys in some back room. When I got back home at ten in the morning she was gone.

I asked my mother what had happened to my wife. Mom said that she came up, complained that I didn't love her, packed her things and had left. At that time she was pregnant, her third month.

She came back six months later to Hartford to have her baby and stayed with my mother until she was able to get around on her own. I was in Florida at the time, so Mom took care of everything.

She wanted a divorce and so we got one in Florida less than two years after we were married. I'll never forget what the judge told me. He said, "Willie Pep, I'm going to grant you this divorce, but you can never bother this woman or see the baby as long as you live."

I have never seen the baby or heard from her since the divorce. It's been fifteen years. My mother keeps telling me that someday the boy will look me up. I hope so.

In the early sixties, I married for the fourth time. I was associated with a nightclub on 57th Street in New York City called Melody Lane. There was a beautiful girl working there as a hat-check girl and I got hooked on her after a couple of months. So I married again. She was a part time actress and working the club at nights to support herself. After I married her she became a full-time actress looking for a part and attending acting classes.

This was my shortest marriage- it lasted less than a year. After quite a few squabbles she landed a part in a road show and we parted. I'm not sure, but I think the touring play was called *Happy Hunting*, a play that Ethel Merman did on Broadway. Anyway, I wished her "good hunting."

However, in one of my marriages, I had moved out of the apartment and decided one day to go back and pick up some of my belongings. When I got there I saw a couple of moving guys taking furniture out of the apartment. When I asked them what they were doing, one of them said, "Oh, we bought all this furniture-the lady sold us all this stuff when she was moving." I seldom got to keep much of any of my furniture that I had bought.

I don't know who was to blame for all the divorces, but a lot of it I suspect was due to a conflict in careers. Two careers are hard on marriages.

An old-timer once told me that if you like being with someone then be with them. If you don't, get away and don't waste your time because life is not so long that you can afford to be unhappy.

Anyway, I have been married now for seven years and I'm very happy with my wife Gerri and my little Melissa.

Getting back to Frankie, at the institute they gave him an electric wheelchair and soon he was wheeling his way into speech therapy class. You see, the speech centers of his brain were okay, but the nerves to his tongue were damaged. So they had to teach him new ways to make sounds. His voice was a murmur but it was a sound and its sound in his ears built his confidence.

Frankie was full speed ahead to get going. I guess it's just something about fighters. I think there's something special about most of them. Anyway, Frankie went to the exercise room and tried to teach himself to walk between the bars that they use. This is really tough because he's only got the use of one arm to balance himself.

Now, it just happened that President Kennedy's father was in the Institute recovering from a stroke. One day the President and Mrs. Kennedy stopped to see Frankie to cheer him up. The President was a real fight fan and had seen several of Frankie's television fights. That visit had to help.

Eighteen months after the accident Frankie wheeled his way out of the hospital. But he still hadn't quit and that determined Irishman finally did teach himself how to walk. No one had hoped for so much, except Frankie Ryff. It was a miracle, they said. Maybe it was. But most of the credit goes to Frankie. It was that big Irish heart that wouldn't quit. After that he spent another stretch in the Bronx Veterans Hospital where his left arm was finally straightened out and some movement restored.

It's been ten years now since the accident and Frankie still improves every day. He now drives a standard car, goes dancing, exercises daily, and generally lives the life he knew. He got married not long ago, to a devoted girl. They met a couple of years ago, dancing at Roseland in New York City. Ironically, Marie lived nearby Frankie in the Bronx. All good things come from the Bronx.

As I said, for therapy, Frankie decided that dancing would be good for him, and he started going to Roseland on Friday nights. Frankie said that to ask a girl to dance isn't so hard. "I couldn't talk too well but I could make motions." Even though he couldn't walk perfectly on the dance floor he was okay. He didn't find it that hard to get dances. "I'm far from being Tyrone Power but I'm no Bugs Bunny."

Well, that's Frankie Ryff. He didn't get to be lightweight champion of the world, though he may have had the ability. But maybe not. Fate cheated him of his final shot at it. But then it doesn't matter. In his heart he's a champ and in my book he's the all-time champion of the world. Yeah, when it came to that real showdown Frankie came out to be "the toughest of 'em all."

ROUND 4

"BABY FACE"

NOT EVERYBODY COMES FROM NEW YORK. Tony Janiro came from a poor neighborhood in Youngstown, Ohio, that made the slums of New York look like Beverly Hills. This was that baby faced kid they used to call "Baby Face." I hadn't seen or heard from Tony in over a year, since the boxing benefit we both attended in New Rochelle, New York. He put on a great boxing exhibition that night. He always was a great boxer.

Tony, at age sixteen, carrying an old valise and an extra pair of overalls and twenty-five bucks, came to New York and started fighting professionally under the wing of Frankie Jacobs. This was in 1942, after Tony had had about sixty-five amateur bouts around the Youngstown area. From the start Tony was a classic boxer, something that seemed to come natural for him with out really trying.

Johnny Greco was his first Garden main event. That was in 1944, I think. He fought Greco three times but only beat him once, which cost him a title shot. Tony never did get a title bout but he came close. If he had beaten Johnny Greco in their third match, he would have had a crack at the then welterweight champion, Freddie "Red" Cochran.

In 1947, on national television, Tony stopped former lightweight champ Beau Jack on a TKO. Jack had hit the canvas with his knee and could not continue. It was a good win for Tony and a tough break for

Beau. They were a lot alike. Both of them made a lot of money and blew it and retired broke. Today Beau is in Florida, where he lives and operates a shoe shine parlor in one of the luxury hotels. Beau's happy; he's got lots of friends and that's important to him. And he makes a damn good living with his shoe shine parlor. At fifty-two, he's as strong as ever. He is the father of fifteen children, five between the ages of nine and fourteen who still live at home. Beau's glory is his children and that's a good life.

Because the middleweight division was so popular at the time, Tony figured it was lucrative to box middleweights. So Tony, a natural welterweight started fighting middleweights and he proved himself in one way by his paychecks.

1947 was a big year for Tony. Besides Beau Jack, Tony had a big Garden bout with Jake LaMotta. Tony, a light-welterweight, was fighting probably one of the toughest middleweights ever. Anyway, in keeping with his idea of fighting middleweights for bigger paychecks, this particular bout started as a joke.

Tony and his manager Frankie Jacobs were at the Garden one day to look for a match and Jake LaMotta just happened to be there for the same reason. Jake in those days was unbeatable and nobody, but nobody, wanted to fight him. He was hungry and looking for fights. Anyway, kidding back and forth, Jake proposed a bout with Tony and guaranteed that he would make 155 pounds. Jake put up $15,000 as a forfeit against the weight limit of 155. So what started out as a joke turned out to be the real thing. A fight was on. Jake made the weight and beat Tony in a ten round decision. The gross at the gate was exceptional because of the popularity, something Jake had counted on.

Tony's fight strategy was to beat Jake on points to keep moving and not just stand there head-on. It's an obvious strategy. How else would anybody beat Jake but on points. But Tony didn't do too bad, considering after the fight he said, "I never had much of a punch. I'd haul off and hit Jake with my best punch smack on the chin and he would just laugh at me." Then that was Jake; one week fighting welterweights and the next light-heavyweights. After a tough fight with Jake his body blows would make most guys pass blood.

From 1942-1951, Tony fought them all, including Kid Gavilan, Charlie Fusari, Umberto Zavala, Tony Pellone, Rocky Graziano and

Rocky Castellani. He had 125 bouts, losing 12 of them, and he grossed about $650,000 total. Not bad for a kid from the slums of Youngstown, Ohio.

Yet, when Tony quit in 1951 he was broke and had to borrow a couple of hundred bucks to pay his rent. At the age of twenty-five, Tony was washed up. Now here's a guy who had sixteen big Garden fights during his colorful career and ends up broke. What happened? Well, he wasn't too thrifty. As Tony would say, it was a case of "Slow horses, fast women and bad booze." I guess when you have money and you're a handsome guy like Tony, the dames are just waiting for you. You're the most beautiful guy in the world-when you've got a buck.

Tony used to walk around with six or seven thousand bucks in his pocket, like it was nothing. His manager, Frankie, always tried to slow him down, and finally managed to convince Tony that he should have at least a checking account. Frankie figured that most of the places that Tony went to knew him and would take his check. So anyway, Tony gave Frankie five thousand bucks to start a checking account. Well, Tony had a new toy –a checkbook. He thought it was great. For Tony it was like giving away paper. A guy asks him for $500 and he would give him some paper. That's how he thought. In about 5 days the checks started the Jersey bounce. In the first week he signed away about $12,000 worth of paper and Frankie gave up. He figured Tony would be better off with cash in his pockets.

In 1952, a year after his retirement, Tony needed money and agreed to fight Charles Humez in Paris, France. Tony was drinking a lot of scotch and had ballooned to 175 pounds. But after six days of steam baths he pruned down to 154. He got beat by Humez but netted himself about $7,000.

When he got back home, he paid off a few debts and ran into a pal who gave him a horse running at Narragansett. Now, Tony had $5000 left over and some temptations. So he gave the money to his wife to hold, telling her that if he asks for it don't give it to him, no matter what. However, after some pleading, his wife gave him the $5000. Tony's pal also had a big Caddy, and along with two other guys they went to the track. They each bet $5000 on the "sure" horse, a total of $20,000. "Can't lose, Tony," his pal kept saying. Well, the horse lost and so did Tony. This guy goes all the way to France to get his brains beat for a paycheck and then throws it away in one fast swoop. The four of them were left with thirty-five cents in their pockets after the race, so when they stopped at a diner and ordered three cups of coffee (with two guys sharing a cup) all they left the waitress was a nickel tip.

Tony lost a lot of money on horses, maybe $100,000. When people know you and you're at the track, you can get twelve tips a race. Since a boxer has a lot of spare time on his hands, and if you like the fresh air, you'll probably wind up at the track. Personally, I like the track and I think if I hadn't become a boxer I would have been a jockey, or at least a tout. It's a nice place to be if you can handle your money. Living in Connecticut, I found it very easy to get to six or seven tracks. In a radius of about 120 miles from my home in Wethersfield there are Lincoln Downs and Narragansett in Providence, Rhode Island, Rockingham in New Hampshire, Suffolk Downs near Boston and a couple in New York. So I used to go to the track quite a bit. I won and lost quite a bit of money myself but it's easy to get hooked chasing that money you lost. Of course, Tony would go to the track with big money and after the first two races he'd try to get his money back.

I once thought owning a race horse would change my luck but it didn't happen. In the early fifties a friend of mine owed me some money and every time I would see him at the track I would ask when he would pay it back. So finally, one day he said, "Gee, Willie, I own five horses. Pick out any one you like." He owed me about $4000 and he wasn't doing too good and so I told him okay I would. I picked out a horse called Gay Spangle, a five year-old filly. So this evened us. I ran the horse about a dozen times during the next year and won about four. I would say I just about broke even. At the time, considering the feed bill, upkeep and the doctor bills, it was costing me, but I put Gay Spangle in a "claiming" race and gave her up.

In the early fifties I was training in Miami, Florida, and would stop in Jake LaMotta's nightclub in Miami Beach. One Sunday night I came in and told Jake that tomorrow I had a day off and probably I'd go to the track. His waitress heard me and asked if she could come since it was her day off also. I told her it was okay with me. Jake said, "if you are going to the racetrack tomorrow, I want you to bet a double for me." On his wall he had photographs of athletes and so he picked out Eddie Arcaro, number one, and Joe DiMaggio, number five. He said to bet one and five for a fifty-dollar double. Then I told the waitress to pick me up at twelve o'clock and not to be late; this would give us plenty of time, at least an hour before post time. So the next day I'm waiting on Collins Avenue with my bartender friend Vic for the waitress at twelve o'clock, and she doesn't show. Then twelve thirty and still no waitress. Finally at one o'clock, half an hour before post time, she pulls up in her car. She apologized and said that the car wouldn't start. Anyway, we get in her car and rush to the track. As soon as we walked through the gate the horses for the first race broke from theirs. And sure enough number one won. Now Jake wanted me to bet a fifty-dollar double on one and five and one had won in the first race. I kept pacing around thinking about what to do since we missed the first race and the waitress on my heels saying, "You know, Jake wanted us to bet the fifty-dollar double." What are you going to do?" So I took the fifty dollars and bet it on number five in the second race for Jake. Sure enough, number five won.

If we had bet the double on time Jake would have won about $4500. It paid real good. As it was we got about $350 for the second race. I said to the waitress to go back and tell Jake that we didn't make the double on time and give him his $350. She said "Will you come back with me and tell him what happened? You know the way he is."

That night we walked in the club and Jake was there. He didn't know what happened. In fact, I don't think he knew what horses he bet. So I said, "Jake, the girl picked me up too late and we missed the first race and I bet the fifty to win on the second race for you and won $350." He said if that's the truth, it's okay and let's forget about it.

The very next day, and for the two weeks that followed, all I heard was that I cheated him out of the winning double. He was on the Gloria DeHaven talk show and he told it. He was on some radio show and he would tell how he got cheated by Willie Pep. The last straw was when I saw it in the papers. So I finally got back to Jake and told him that he had to stop telling this story about me winning the double and not paying him. People were starting to believe him and it bothered me. "Don't worry, Willie, the story makes for good listening and good publicity," Jake says.

Jake had a very nice club in Miami, and one day he took me upstairs to the club's office to show me how smart he was. He said, "I'm a pretty smart guy and nobody puts one over on me in my place." We went into the men's room in his office, toward the medicine cabinet on the wall. He pushed the cabinet over like you see in a mystery picture and said for me to take a look. Well, through that cabinet I saw the whole floor of the club. "See, Willie, nobody gives me the business. I know what's going on in my joint all the time.

So when I got back downstairs I tell all the bartenders and waiters that Jake could see every move with his trick medicine cabinet and pointed to the spot. Jake wasn't very happy with that, but what the hell, it makes for good listening and good publicity.

When most fighters quit it takes a year for them to go broke, but for Tony Janiro he had to go to work right away. His manager, Jacobs, who owned the Neutral Corner at 55th Street and 8th Avenue, gave Tony a job bartending. There was Tony behind the bar and on the other side was the same guys he was picking up tabs for. At first, Tony was embarrassed, especially when his former friends would leave a tip at the bar. It took a little time for him to get used to it, but a guy has to eat.

Bartending has been the job for Tony in lots of places since his retirement. He once took a tavern on a trial basis with the option to buy after a year's time. Well, he built it up so good that the guy sold it right from under him before the year was up and made himself a sizeable profit. There are guys who pick up lots of bars, opened or closed, and then have guys with names like Tony to build them up. They make all sorts of promises and then give you the royal screw. That's the lot for lots of ex-fighters.

Tony was the kind of guy that could stay out all night and fight a ten-rounder the next day, and win. He would make the rounds of all the night spots with his so called pals and pick up all the tabs. I guess the only one who understood Tony was his wife. Married for twenty-six years, they're still together today and have a twenty-four year old son. For Tony, having a good time with the boys was more than a casual thing. It kept his mind in shape. According to Tony, his mind had to be in better condition than his body. If his mind was in shape, he felt that he could fight better. He always thought his body could take the abuse and it had to. A fighter never gets hit in the mind.

Another natural boxer like Tony was a welterweight by the name of Joe Miceli, who fought for about twelve years. Miceli, a main eventer most of the time, was seen a lot on television and was averaging about fifty or sixty thousand a year during his peak. Joe, who had a tremendous left hook beat the biggies like Gavilan, Saxton, Dykes, Aragon and Ike Williams when he was in shape. His trainer, the late Dan Florio, once said, "He could box like Benny Leonard when he wanted to, slip leads like Lou Ambers and counter like the 'Fargo Express' Billy Petrolle. When he was in shape there wasn't a welterweight in the world who could beat him, and there were damn few middleweights around who could take him either. He had everything but common sense.

He was a lot like Tony. When he got an urge to do something, he did it. Nothing mattered, not even a fight. He really liked good times and that drove his manager and promoters up a tree.

Knowing the finer points of the boxing game and losing a lot of bad decisions, Tony is a firm believer that the referee should never be allowed to judge a fight. It leads to bad decisions and lots of guys getting hurt. He's got a point. The referee has got too much on his mind and his main role is protecting the two guys in the ring. Yet there are some who think that the referee has the best view of the bout and therefore should be the sole judge of a fight. Tony talks about his friend, welterweight Jimmy Doyle, who was boxing Ray Robinson in 1949 in Cleveland, a non-title fight. It was a very good fight until Ray hit Jimmy with a combination and down he went; his head bounced off the canvas. Jimmy Doyle died the next day. Now Jimmy had taken a tremendous beating in a bout with Artie Levine before the Robinson bout. Artie beat Doyle bad and gave him a concussion. The referee should have stopped it but he was too occupied tallying up points, judging the fight. The Robinson fight, which was billed as a comeback for Jimmy, just put the finishing touches on Levine's work.

Usually it's the fight before that sets the stage for the accident and usually it's a fight that should have been stopped. Benny "Kid" Paret took a great deal of punishment from Gene Fullmer prior to the Emile Griffith Bout. And the same was so with Primo Carnera against Ernie Schaaf in the thirties - Max Baer had set the stage for the Schaaf accident.

In spite of all the money Tony made, he still owes the Federal Government $20,000 in taxes from his ring earnings, and this goes back to 1950 with the interest still pilin up. Tony just about makes it with his bartending wages and can't afford to pay it back. "Maybe," says Tony, "if I hit on a lottery ticket I can pay it back." He thinks the Government can wait.

The fight game is not like a regular job where taxes are withheld from your weekly paycheck. In boxing, the boxer gets the gross check and no taxes are taken out. How can you know what your tax is supposed to be before you pay your manager, trainer and take out for expenses! The tax is based on the net earnings. Anyway, with this wrinkle, a boxer sometimes forgets to declare his taxes on time and uses it for something else.

In the late forties, if anyone told Tony that he would be working for a living, he'd say you were crazy. I guess most fighters feel the same way; Rocky Graziano. He never went broke. He was smart. Lots of guys like Rocky had a knack for managing their money. He also had some luck. As Rocky recently said, "My manager, Irving Cohen, kept paying into an annuity for me and when I quit fighting, I was going to go to Miami and open a bar. It was a $100,000 annuity, and it's worth about $300,000 now. But then Nat Hiken, a big TV guy, got me a job as Martha Raye's boyfriend on her TV show, and I kept going." I guess Tony and myself never had that so-called knack or luck, and blew it away. Some guy could go out and spend twenty bucks and look like he's got all the class in the world. Another guy could go for two thousand bucks and look like a bum.

Still a young man at forty-seven, Tony now lives a quiet life with his wife and has an apartment in Manhattan. If you want to stop by and say hello to Tony, he has been working for six years at Tom and Sal's Tavern at 172nd Street and St. Nicholas Avenue. You can't miss that ".".

ROUND 5

"Trial Horse"

Literally beaten from pillar to post by an unranked, unruffled plodder named Tiger Jones, a sadder but wiser Sugar Ray Robinson began a 10 day cooling out period in which he will decide whether or not to hang up the red leather mittens for good

Gene Ward—New York Daily News—1955

With Ginks' help we finally got into Secaucus and parked in the diner's lot across the street from Al Certo's Custom Tailor Shop. When I got out of my Caddy, I heard a guy a guy call my name. It was Tiger Jones. The other guys, Tippy Larkin, Charley Fusari and Ernie Durando hadn't arrived as yet. Ginks and I, and Tiger went in the diner for some coffee. Talking with Tiger, I couldn't help but think back about the way this man could fight. He was never a champ but he was certainly one of the best.

Tiger's childhood was pretty tough. He was born in Brooklyn in 1928 and was brought up through the Depression. Tiger was one of ten kids, which didn't help matters. He ended up spending more time at the children's shelter, the Association for the Prevention of Cruelty to Children, than at home. At nineteen, he moved to Queens and, and not having much else to do, he started boxing at the P.A.L. Gil Clancy

 45

was working with the kids there and he saw something in Tiger. As a result, he took him under his wing, which was the break for Tiger. Now Gil never did manage Tiger as a pro, which was a shame because Tiger became just about as popular a fighter as you could be, though he was always getting the short end of decisions and just missing the big pay days.

The Tiger deserved his popularity. It was always true that a Tiger fight was an exciting fight. Tiger always came to fight, and he would make the other guy fight or chase him right out of the ring, and this included the very best of the welterweights and middleweights. He beat some of them, and he lost to some of them, but every one of them knew he was in a fight. And the fans loved it. Tiger's audience was pretty large because out of his eighty-nine pro bouts, sixty-three were on TV and thirty-five of them were on national TV. That's more TV fights than any other boxer in the business.

The boxing fans of the fifties knew the fighters, knew their styles and knew the fights they wanted to see. Tiger was one of the favorites because aside from action they also appreciated boxing skills, and those skills of Tiger Jones. The TV fight fan of the fifties was no different from the rabid fans of earlier years, except they were able to form more of their own opinions because they could *see* the fight and not rely solely on the voice of some sportscaster. They had the chance of seeing about two hundred main events each year on television, and just about every ranking fighter in America. You name the day, they had a fight-Monday night fights, Tuesday night, Wednesday, Thursday, and, of course, the most popular, the Friday night fights. And also the Saturday night fights. At times, I think the whole country was watching the fights and drinking beer.

But Tiger's popularity didn't happen overnight. He had fifty-five amateur fights and, like most kids, he was boxing purely for sport at first and never thought of money. But things were tough and after having six different jobs and six months of unemployment in one year, he decided to give pro fighting two years.

Tiger didn't waste any time. Two years after turning pro he came close to upsetting Johnny Saxton who was undefeated at the time. That was in October of 1952 in a ten rounder at St. Nick's in New York. Now most of the fans thought Tiger won, even though

Willie Pep at age 5

Wilie Pep at age 9

 47

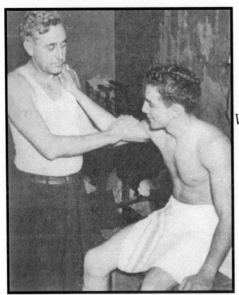

Willie with Trainer Bill Gore

Willie Pep at age 16 – Connecticut Amateur Champion

 48

Willie wins title from Chalky Wright – November 20, 1942 N.Y. Daily News

Willie with Bandleader Harry James after winning title

Willie in the Navy - 1943

Willie in the Army – 1945 with Tami Mauriello

Willie Retains title against Phil Terranova (R) - 1945   N.Y. *Daily News*

Ruby Goldstein counts out Sal Bartolo in 1946 – Willie retains title
N.Y. *Daily News*

 51

A stiff right by Willie sets France's Ray Famechon on his heels in 1950-Willie retained title   N.Y. *Daily News*

"Believe it or Not" Coley Welch down for the 3rd time with one Belloise punch- 1945-N.Y. Daily News

Orlando Zulueta (R) hits with a left to Frankie Ryff's head - 1954
Photos N.Y. Daily News

A jarring right by Belloise to the jaw of bloody Robert Villemain - 1949
Photos N.Y. Daily News

Ryff with Chester Rico (L) at the Roseland Dance City -1971

Ryff in Wheelchair with Chico Vejar - 1963
Photos N.Y. Daily News

 55

Beau Jack (L) and Tony Janiro 1947   N.Y. Daily News

Tiger Jones lands right to Johnny Bratton's (R) jaw - 1952   N.Y. Daily News

Tiger Jones beats Sugar Ray Robinson - 1955
N.Y. Daily News

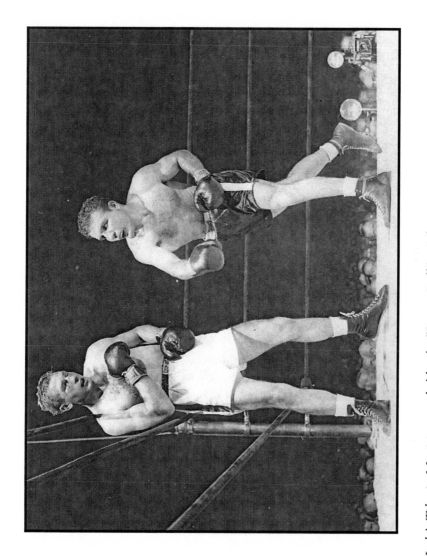

Italy's Tiberio Mitri is pounded by the "Bronx Bull" – Jake LaMotta - 1950   N.Y. Daily News

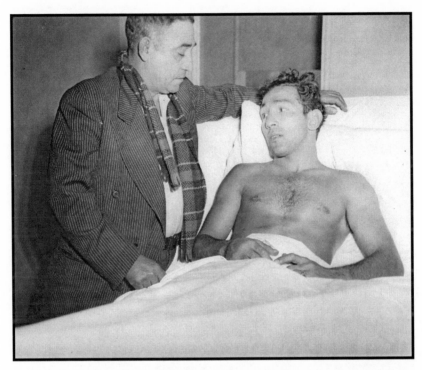

Willie with his Dad after plane accident - 1947   N.Y. Daily News

Tony Canzoneri, Barney Ross, Joey Adams, Mickey Walker and Benny Leonard during World War II

Sandy Saddler stops Willie and wins title - 1948   N.Y. Daily News

Sandy Saddler vs. Willie Pep in NY's Madison Square Garden in their 2nd bout held on Feb. 11th 1949 for the Featherweight Championship of the World —Willie wins back his title with a 15 round decision   N.Y. Daily News

Willie fights his greatest fight and regains title from Saddler– 1949   N.Y. Daily News

Willie fights his greatest fight - 1949   N.Y. Daily News

Willie drops Saddler in 3rd fight – 1950   N.Y. Daily News

Willie loses title to Saddler in their 3rd fight - 1950   N.Y. Daily News

Willie shoots a jab to Saddler's heart   N.Y. Daily News

Referee Ray Miller is down
N.Y. Daily News

Willie and Sandy all wrapped up   N.Y. Daily News

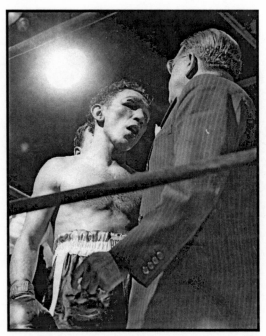

Dr. Nardiello is checking Willie's eye instead of looking up his nose - 1951
N.Y. Daily News

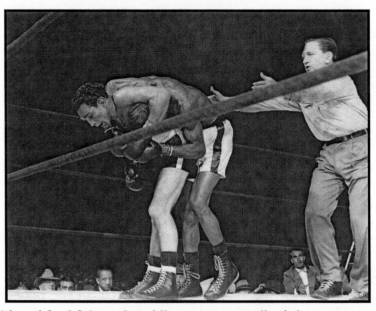

4th and final fight with Saddler in 1951 — Willie fails to regain title
N.Y. Daily News

Willie is hitch-hiking on Sandy's back 4th and final fight with Saddler in 1951 – Willie Fails to Regain the title

N.Y. Daily News

"Bad Boy" Joey Giardello tags Dick Tiger.
Tiger regains middleweight title - 1965   N.Y. Daily News

Graham knocks Gavilan's eyeballs into corner pocket. - Gavilan wins disputed title decision - 1951   N.Y. Daily News

Gavilan beats Johnny Bratton for Welterweight title – 1950
N.Y. Daily News

he had been a ten to one underdog. Tiger gave Saxton a good fight, but if you're going to beat a guy who's undefeated and being promoted by Blinky Palermo you've just about got to destroy him.

Tiger had his days when he could do just that. In December, right after the Saxton fight, he fought Johnny Bratton. The International Boxing Club was looking for a good opponent for Bratton, the former welterweight champion, who was being rebuilt by the powers that be. They needed someone who would give a good show but that Bratton could handle easily. Tiger seemed to them to be perfect.

At ringtime you couldn't get a bet on Bratton at any price and a guy could have written his own ticket if he liked Jones. Now this was a ten rounder at the Garden, a big fight, national television. Bratton was the kind of guy who liked to set his own pace, but the Tiger wouldn't let him. He kept boring in. He took his best shots and still staggered Bratton several times. Tiger came to fight and he kept the pressure on. The fight was so one-sided that there was no way he could lose. He was a four to one underdog, but he beat Bratton bad in a one-sided decision. At one time, people said Tiger's manager, Bobby Melnick, had put him in over his head, but Tiger showed them and the exposure on national TV was great for him. Tiger loved television.

They used to say that Johnny Bratton had a glass jaw because he had it fractured three times, the last being with Kid Gavilan when the Kid beat him for the welterweight title in 1951. But it wasn't so. The jaw breaks were caused by an impacted wisdom tooth so that a baby could have broken his jaw. He had the tooth extracted and his jaw problems were over. This was well before he fought Tiger....Johnny's later troubles didn't come from his jaw.

Tiger went on to fight the best- Ray Robinson, Kid Gavilan, Gene Fullmer, Joey Giardello, Bobo Olson, Bobby Dykes and half dozen or more foreign champions. He was always right up there with the big boxing figures and in big fights. The fights presumably were always for the other guy's career, not Tiger's. Promoters would be looking past him, so they came out on top if he would lose. Tiger says he always was getting the short end of the stick; if he didn't win decisively he would lose the decision. He never was awarded a close fight. Of his thirty-one losses, a lot of people feel well over half of those decisions could have gone Tiger's way.

In 1955 he fought Joey Giambra in Dallas, Texas, on national TV. When Giambra got the decision it was so bad that fans were calling in from all over the country about it. Another time he fought Bobby Dykes at Eastern Parkway arena in Brooklyn. Dykes was a big favorite to win. Now the fight was close, and Tiger knew he didn't have much of a chance in a close fight, so he really went to work in the tenth round and he dropped Dykes twice with overhand rights to the chin. Now there were forty-eight seconds to go, which was too long for Dykes and the referee had to stop it. Sure enough the officials' cards had Tiger Jones losing bad. Tiger is a strong believer in that the fight officials are influenced by their own betting or pressures put on them and they judge accordingly. It sure is hard to explain what's going on sometimes.

In those days' most foreign champs who came over had to get by Tiger before they got a crack at the title or even just another big fight; that way the matchmaker got two gates, one with Tiger and one with the main guy. Since Tiger didn't get much, there was a lot to go around after the first fight, and then the foreigner would have that good TV exposure, beating Tiger fresh in everybody's mind, which would push up the gate for the second fight. Of course this all depended on Tiger cooperating by losing.

Tiger fought the Argentinian champ, Eduardo Lausse, at Madison Square Garden in 1955. Tiger was a two to one underdog. Now Lausse was a good, tough fighter who could take his opponent out with a left hook. He had just won twenty-seven straight, twenty-one by knockout. But the Tiger worked him over real good and he was cut bad. Up to the eighth round Tiger was ahead on points. Three times Dr. Vincent Nardiello came into the ring and recommended that they stop the fight because Lausse's eye cuts were so bad. But the referee wouldn't hear of it. In the ninth round, Tiger had Lausse pinned up against the ropes for forty-five seconds, pounding him, but he wouldn't go down. Tiger, he kept looking for the referee to stop it, but he didn't. Tiger couldn't believe it.

Tiger went back to his corner before the tenth and he told his manager that he didn't think that he could win the fight. He was right; the decision came in and it was unanimous for Lausse. Not even close. Dr. Nardiello ordered Lausse to St. Claire's Hospital where they had to put thirty-two stitches in his face. Could the referee have been hitting Lausse?

Tiger gave everybody a good fight. He had three of them with Kid Gavilan, three split decisions, too, and winning only one of them. He split two other fights with Joey Giardello and lost two decisions to Gene Fullmer from West Jordan, Utah. Now they were all world champions and Tiger gave them all a good fight. Professionally, Tiger has no kind words for Gene Fullmer.

"In my opinion he stunk," he says. "He couldn't fight. He would aggravate a guy with his unorthodox style. When he beat Robinson, Ray didn't want to win. He hurt Fullmer several times, staggered him, and then grabbed him to hold him up. I'm sure that Ray was looking for a rematch to make more money."

Anyway, in the rematch Robinson knocked him out very early. That was hard to do, too. Gene seldom got hit solid because he was always moving and charging his opponents.

But the big thing wasn't Jones vs. Fullmer or Robinson vs. Fullmer. The big thing that they still talk about is the fight Tiger had with Ray in 1955. Sugar Ray as the welterweight champ moved to the middleweights and won the title by battering Jake LaMotta. Ray was going along beating everybody, but he was getting on a little bit. When he decided to shoot for the light-heavyweight title against champion Joey Maxim he was thirty-one or thirty-two. That June night in 1952 was hot and steaming with lots of humidity. Ray was winning on points, but failed to come out for the fourteenth round. His fast pace coupled with the weather exhausted him.

After that Ray became a nightclub entertainer, a song and dance man. But he wasn't doing well financially, and being only thirty-four at the time he figured he had enough left for another crack at the middleweight title. Bobo Olson held the title at the time and Ray had beaten him twice, in 1950 and again in 1952.

As part of his comeback, they picked Tiger Jones, naturally. Tiger had lost his five previous fights before Robinson, but all were the usual split or bad decisions. Ray was a six to one favorite and the fight was on national television. To everyone's surprise, Tiger gave Ray the worst beating of his career. Pound for pound Ray was one of the greatest boxers of all time, and at that point he had won 141 fights and only lost 3. However, he had never looked so bad. Tiger made him look like an amateur and gave him his fourth loss. Tiger staggered Ray, tore his mouth, and cut him under the eye so badly that his entire face was bloody.

There was talk about a return bout, but they said there were money differences and also Tiger was a problem. They figured that Ray just couldn't beat him. Tiger says the smart money people would have given him a return bout with Ray if he made sure he wouldn't win. But his part of the gate would be only $10,000. The smart money people had the wrong guy, because Tiger was always in there to win.

Besides, he wouldn't have gone down for $10,000. The rematch was never made and as a result Tiger is one up on Ray.

Another time Tiger was to fight Jacques Royer, two-time French middleweight champ, at the Garden. When he was training a guy approached him and offered him $10,000 to lose. Tiger said no. Later the guy came back and upped the offer to $15,000. Tiger told him that if he came back again he was going to go to the commission. After the third round of the fight Tiger's arms hurt so much he couldn't lift them. He hung in there for ten rounds and lost. Now some critics had doubts about the bout. After the fight even the same guy who tried to bribe him showed up and told him what a dummy he was for not taking the money. However, after visiting five doctors Tiger found out that he was anemic and that his blood pressure drops when he starts training. He started taking vitamins and iron shots before his bouts but that still didn't help. He finally went to a chiropractor and the guy straightened out his spine. He was fine after that.

Anyway, fights like that cast an ugly shadow and sometimes you can't do anything about it. I was once accused of a bad fight. I used to train with a guy named Lulu Perez in New York in early 1954. At the time he was an up-and-coming fighter and I was the former champion. I boxed him in the gym and never had any trouble with him. Well, several months later we were matched to fight at the Garden and everybody thought I wouldn't have trouble with him.

I trained for this fight in Florida, and believe me, I was in good shape. Instead of taking a plane or train to New York, I drove the 1500 miles to the fight. That's something you never do. At fight time, I was confident that I would beat him like I used to in the gym.

In the second round, Perez hit me on the chin and knocked me down with a good punch, and after I got up he knocked me down for the second time. He was a good puncher, Lulu. Towards the end of the round he hit me with a going away right hand and knocked me down again. I was up without a count but the referee stopped the fight automatically with the three knockdown rule. I think that the referee should have taken into consideration the fact that if a fighter is not hurt he should be allowed to continue. But he stopped the fight.

The talk after this fight was that I didn't fight and that's bad publicity for any boxer. The facts were that Lulu was a good right hand puncher and he caught me cold. At the time I was thirty-two and had been in the ring for sixteen years. Lulu hit me a couple of good punches and when you're in your thirties you can't take the same punch you did in your twenties. Your body is older and punches hurt a lot more.

I was stopped two years earlier in the Boston Garden by Tommy Collins. As with Perez, I trained with Tommy in the gym and never had problems with him. He had a tremendous right hand punch, but I never had any problems with him inside the gym. Yet in the ring it's a little different than in the gym – a puncher is always a threat. He knocked me down three times in the sixth round and the referee stopped the fight. Now here's a fight I'm glad the referee stopped. I was hurt and who knows what could happen to you when you're groggy and don't know what's going on.

After the Lulu Perez bout, Dr. Vincent Nardiello, the chief medical officer for the New York State Athletic Commission, came into my dressing room to examine me. It was standard procedure to examine a boxer before and after each fight. Anyway, the doctor looks up my nose and says, "Kid, your reflexes are gone. It would be dangerous for you to fight again." I never thought my nose had anything to do with my reflexes; maybe they weren't what they used to be (my reflexes, that is) but they weren't gone, and certainly not up my nose. It didn't sound like medical advice but more like sour grapes for my poor showing against Perez. I had heard that he had a good bit of money on me.

The analysis by Nardiello not only hurt me personally but it put me out of New York—the big fight town. I continued to box outside of New York State, any place that I could. I got some good purses and some bad, but the important thing was that I was boxing and winning. In fact, I won about sixty fights since the doctor looked up my nose in 1954 until my bout with featherweight champ Hogan "Kid" Bassey in 1958. That's more bouts than the average professional boxer has in his entire career, even when his reflexes were not gone.

77

In 1958, I was stopped by the featherweight champ, Hogan "Kid" Bassey, at the Boston Garden. Again Because of knockdowns the referee stopped the bout. I had Bassey for eight rounds, winning seven of the eight, of a ten-round non-title go; but in the ninth round he knocked me down twice and the referee stopped it there. I was really hurt and the referee saw it. If I could have survived the last round, I would have boxed him for the championship of the world.

But like I said, age has a lot to do with boxing. I was almost thirty-eight when I fought Bassey and boxing is really a young man's game. As you get older the rounds seem longer and when you get hit it's just not as easy to come back as it used to be. You keep looking for that extra something in those late rounds and each year you find less and less of it. I had it for the first fifteen years and then it started downhill for me. I retired shortly after the "Kid" Bassey fight, about twenty years after I started. So the outcome of a fight might look a bit strange to a lot of people, including some boxing commissions, but one has to realize that a guy called Father Time finally catches up with you. Though, in Tiger's bout with Royer, it wasn't a case of age, but low blood Pressure.

After Tiger beat Robinson he got to fight Bobo Olson the middleweight champion, in Chicago Stadium. Olson wanted a shot at Archie Moore's light-heavyweight title but had to prove himself by beating former light-heavyweight champ Joey Maxim; and he had to set the stage for that fight by beating no one else but Tiger Jones, and he had to be convincing. And so another situation where Tiger had to come first. Now Olson went in at the heaviest of his career, 168 pounds. As I said before, you could beat Tiger, but you couldn't murder him. So Tiger lost, but he left his marks on Olson; he was definitely in a fight. However, two of the officials scored the fight ten rounds out of ten for Bobo. Most spectators figured that Tiger had definitely won three rounds anyway and that one was even. But Olson won big, as he hoped, and got the shot against Maxim at San Francisco's Cow Palace. Olson then beat Maxim and in the same year he also fought Archie Moore for the title and defended his middleweight crown against Ray Robinson. Archie kayoed Bobo in three rounds and Ray put him away in two. Carl "Bobo" Olson maybe got stopped twice that year, but he also made a lot of money that same year.

Another champion Tiger fought was middleweight Paul Pender. He lost to Paul on points in a tough decision in the Boston Garden. But Tiger says kiddingly, "How do you beat an Irishman in his hometown of Boston on Saint Patrick's Day?" That's no joke, but it sounds like the beginning of one.

So that was Tiger. He was the favorite TV fighter of the fifties, a real Friday Hero. Tiger felt that better management could have given him better purses and the big money the other guys were making. Television isn't really paying the good money for Tiger. Hell, he made more money on fights which weren't televised. He got $10,000 to fight Charley Humez in Paris, $7500 to go against Joey Giambra and $8000 in his last fight against the Austrian champ, Laslo Papp, in Vienna. But a television fight, a national hook-up, got him only $4000 plus a percentage from the small gate, maybe a thousand or so. In his twelve-year career Tiger figures he grossed $150,000 for himself, which isn't a lot for a guy who was constantly fighting the best and entertaining millions of viewers.

Tiger lives in Queens Village now with his pretty wife Cora and three teen-age sons in a two-family house that he bought some years back. Cora is an elementary school teacher in the New York City school system and Tiger runs a fork lift truck for the Continental Can Company. Like a lot of the ex-boxers, Tiger is not happy with his job and would like to get involved with sports-like teaching kids boxing and physical fitness. For Tiger now, it's just bowling but with averages around 195 in an industrial league. Tiger Jones' real name is Ralph, but in the ring it was the Tiger that fought all those great fighters. As I said, it seemed Tiger always had to come first even though it was really Ralph.

ROUND 6

"THE BAD BOY OF BOXING"

FIGHTERS AREN'T ANY DIFFERENT FROM ANYBODY else. Trouble has a way of finding everyone, including them. You've got to remember that many fighters came from tough neighborhoods where trouble's a way of life. Some of them are bound to carry a little of that life with them. One must remember that when they get into fighting these guys are around temptation all the time. As a result, very few go wrong in the ring, no matter what they say. But because they're fighters, every time they get into a scrape outside the ring they make headlines, and even if they devote the rest of their lives to worthwhile things, they're carrying a kind of black mark with them forever. But there were some guys who seemed to go out of their way to help create this kind of image. One former champion had plenty of fights inside the ring that a lot of people questioned. At least the decisions that all went his way. He had lots of help in his corner. But his trouble went beyond the ring apron. One Time his wife had called the cops saying he was threatening to blow her brains out. Though they found a loaded gun hidden in a shoe in his house, the cops let him go.

Another time they got him for a scofflaw. He had a dozen traffic violations and a speeding ticket, I think. They took him to traffic court and the judge fined him $650 and gave him a fifteen-day suspended jail sentence; this was the day after he won the title. So in court, as

the champion, he wore the gloves he wore in the fight, assuming he could cash in on his new publicity. During proceedings he squared off against the traffic summons clerk who was to collect the fine from him. Naturally, the judge got mad and warned him that one more mistake would have him in jail. Now, as a fighter and a champion he should have gone out of his way to keep a thing like that quiet. He didn't.

Another time he got into an argument near his home with two guys over a parked car and they were supposed to have challenged him with jack handles; he went after them with a baseball bat. Now, the papers blew it up and said the guys were unarmed. Now it doesn't matter if this champion was right or wrong; the point is he should have walked away or called a cop at least. Chasing after guys with a baseball bat doesn't do you or the sport any good. Not even baseball.

There were other guys who had trouble. One heavyweight was supposed to have been linked with Detroit's "Purple Gang." Now it may not be true. However, as good listening as it may have been it was still bad publicity. That also goes for a hard hitting heavyweight of the fifties who was picked up for running a whorehouse. The police tagged him with some marked money and our man had it with him when he was arrested.

My point is some guys were definitely out of line. But when they made headlines it looked like everyone in the sport was somehow involved. It seemed that right or wrong, most of us were bad.

Trouble can come in smaller doses as well. For example, only once did I have to hit a guy out of the ring. I was in a nightclub in Hartford with a girl who I'd known for a long time when this guy walks in, someone she had been seeing for a while but had dropped when he got too serious. He walked over to the table and started talking very loud, and then he slapped the girl. I got up. Then I told him that was it for him. So he threw a punch at me, naturally he missed. Then I slapped him, being careful to keep my hand open (being a licensed fighter) and I think I cut his lip. The cops came in and they arrested him for starting the disturbance. He was found guilty and fined.

Yet a week later I found that he was suing me. You see, my hands are weapons, legally. So I went to my lawyer and I told him the whole story and he said its aggravation and that he would find out what the guy wanted. So sure enough he called me back in a couple of days and said that the guy would settle for $1000. The end result was that I gave him the $1000 and $500 for the lawyer; $1500 and I hadn't even really hit him. I had just slapped him but it cut his lip a little bit. What a score that was. A couple of days later the man bought a Buick with the money.

That was the only fight I ever had. I learned that if somebody's fighting I walk out into the street and that's it. I have never had trouble on the street.

But one time I had a place in Tampa, a placed called Willie Pep's Little Club. One night a guy was creating a disturbance at the bar. When I walked over to him he stuck a .45 in my ribs and he said, "Willie Pep, I'm gonna kill ya." So I said, "Let's talk this over," without a smile. I went outside with him and with no idea as to what I was going to do. I tried to talk to him, but he was hopelessly drunk. He had me with my hands up and he was teasing me about how he was going to kill me and that I wasn't that tough after all. Every time I made the slightest move, he would shove this .45 into my ribs. I was praying this guy was only trying to scare me. I got lucky. A police cruiser came by and arrested him. I don't know what happened to the guy. I never pressed charges. I was luckier than some guys, both with this guy and the press.

But with all the bad press that boxing gets, not much is written about the charity work of guys like Marciano, Vejar, Louis and Zale. And what about the kids that boxing straightened out. It is not a short list. But the guy's life that sums up this whole problem has got to be Joey Giardello's. Joey may have had a little wild streak in him but he's the salt of the earth. He had a lot of tough times and sometimes it was his fault; but usually it was just a case of bad luck. But, whatever the case, the papers always jumped on him. Once, when he was on crutches, he got arrested for supposedly attacking a gas station attendant with his crutch. At the time Joey had a clean record, yet he got six to eighteen months probably with the help of the papers. "The Bad Boy of Boxin'," they called him. It was ridiculous, but that's what he had to fight, and because of it had a rough career. Yet, he put more into boxing than it could possibly give back. Joey was not without courage; for every piece of tough luck he got, he gave back something good of himself. For that I have a great deal of respect for the man, Joey Giardello.

Joey was born Carmine Tellelli in Brooklyn in 1930. He was always easygoing and also easily talked into things. That's been part of his trouble. Anyway, when he was fifteen and a half a buddy talked him into joining the Army. To get around the age problem they borrowed a Baptismal certificate of a guy named Joey Giardello. Carmine Tellelli has never met Joey Giardello. Anyway, Joey, who had never fought as a kid accept in the streets, took up boxing at Fort Bragg, North Carolina, when he found out that the winners got a three-day pass. Joey did all right and after his discharge in 1948 he went to Philadelphia to train and turn professional.

Well, Joey fought in the service for something. My service was different. In 1943, all my friends were joining up and I decided to join the Army. I went down to the induction board in Hartford and told them I wanted to join the Army. On the way a Lieutenant Commander for the Navy saw me and asked where I was going. I told him that I was going to join the Army, and he said, "Willie, why don't you join the Navy? It's a better life. You'll like it and you'll probably be sent with the boxing team, maybe to become the boxing instructor. We need guys like you. So I joined the Navy.

However, when I went through their medical they found a perforated eardrum, so after basic training they put me with the football team instead of the boxing team. They made me water boy for the football team. Me, the featherweight champion of the world. Well, they wanted their water and I ran out with two buckets. All the football players knew me and they'd say, "Willie, what are you doin' here?" and I'd tell them that this is where I'm best serving the Navy. It never got a laugh. This lasted for about one season, when I was finally shipped to Bainbridge, Maryland, to train as a "Boatsman Mate." After a year or so in the Navy I was finally discharged because of that perforated eardrum. With the cold weather in Bainbridge, the ear always gave me lots of trouble; and so I never saw a boxing glove in the Navy. Joey always had a better ear than I did.

In 1946, after being out almost a year, I got my induction papers to go into the Army. I went down to the induction center and said that I was in the Navy before and if I had to go back in I wanted the Navy. I learned that the Navy didn't want me, and so I was drafted into the Army and assigned to Cushing General Hospital in Framingham, Massachusetts.

I was an M.P. in the hospital. There were a lot of wounded guys and some others who either went A.W.O.L. or did something else. We had a jailhouse with three or four cells. When I came in the morning I would unlock the cell doors and let the prisoners answer all the phone calls for me while I was lounging around. It was a soft touch for me. This lasted for almost a year until my discharge. Over two years in the service and I never saw a boxing glove, yet for Joey his service was the beginning of his fight career.

Joey had his first big fight in December, 1952. He beat Billy Graham in a ten-round decision at Madison Square Garden. It was a great fight and drew the largest crowd ever at that time for a non-title fight, with a gate of around $90,000.

He almost lost this fight when the New York Boxing Commission tried to reverse it; but he took it to court and won it back. After that he was dodged by a lot of guys - Olson, Robinson and Basilio stayed away from him and the following year he lost to Billy Graham and to Johnny Saxton in a fight where one judge had six rounds even. Saxton's manager was Blinky Palermo and Blinky was big in Philadelphia where the fight was held. That's a lot of help in your corner.

Joey could box, punch, and move with grace. He was a great middleweight and big things were predicted for him in his early days. In 1954 he started out with three knockouts in a row and it looked like he was on his way. Then the roof caved in. He was in an automobile accident and ended up on crutches. And that service station incident happened during an election year in Philadelphia with the district attorney running for mayor. The result was that Joey spent most of 1955 in Jail. He didn't fight from March, 1955, until February, 1956, which in those days was a long layoff. Now you can imagine how he felt; he had been clean and now he had a record. He was miserable and his career looked like it might be over.

At this time he and his wife Rosalie found out that their son, Carmen was retarded; he was a Mongoloid. Even today, people don't know much about the retarded and then even less. Finding it in your own home was a terrific shock. With everything else, Joey went into a tailspin.

But Joey, being Joey, was down but not out. It took him a while, but he fought back, all the way to the championship. Joey's retired now, but not from life; he's built a new life out of helping other youngsters like his son.

But I'm getting ahead of myself. Joey took a long time to get all the way back; he fought a lot of fights and did well, but couldn't get a

 84

shot at the title until 1960 when he fought Gene Fullmer, in one of the roughest fights anyone ever saw.

Gene, being champion, dictated the conditions and got a small ring. Now, Joey liked to keep moving while Gene liked to corner a guy; when they fought Gene kept charging and butting and after a while Joey did the same. The fight was called a draw by the officials. A lot of guys picked on Fullmer for being dirty in the ring but the problem was that Gene didn't have a classic boxing style and knew very little about the finer points of the game. He was awkward and his forte was his strength and determination to win. It was the only way he knew.

After the Fullmer bout it began to look bad for Joey. He had lost three straight and they were starting to say he was all washed up and ought to quit. But then Dick Tiger beat Fullmer and was recognized as the champion when Paul Pender retired. Joey knew that Tiger was the type of guy who barred no challenger. Since they had fought twice before, each winning one, Joey saw the possibility of another chance. He was thirty-three and had been fighting for fifteen years with 114 bouts. He was very close to retiring. But now his ambition was revived and he went to work. He won nine of his next eleven and was on three straight when they booked him to fight Ray Robinson. Ray was thirty-eight or thirty-nine, this was in 1962, and commentators were saying that they both should quit and that this fight would prove it. Joey thought differently. He beat Ray badly, one of the few to ever do that, despite Robinson's age.

Beating Ray led to a championship fight with Dick Tiger in 1963 in Atlantic City. He was a three to one underdog going in, but he still won the championship from Tiger.

Now being champ, Joey was flooded with offers from promoters, even from Madison Square Garden; the guys at the Garden had ignored Joey for eight years because of his "record." The Garden people went as far as getting Joey his license back; yes, how success changes everything for a guy when he's on top. Today, it makes no difference if you're an ex- convict or even a draft dodger- you get a fight.

So Joey was champion at thirty-three. Two years later, in 1965, he defended against Dick Tiger in a return. Tiger beat him, and while Joey stayed pretty active for ten more fights in the next three years, he retired in 1968 at the age of thirty-eight; it was pretty much over.

But Joey didn't have anything more to prove. He had 139 fights with 111 wins, 21 losses, and 7 draws. He had made well over a million dollars and had some money when he quit. He lived good; but he learned from his dad that "your family comes first." He never forgot.

Joey was a frustrated baseball player who loved to play softball whenever he got a chance. This drove his manager crazy, especially when he played on concrete. One time when Joey was set to box Kid Gavilan he went and cracked his arm in a softball game. The bout was called off and he never did get another shot at Gavilan. Another time at the East Orange, New Jersey, training camp Joey organized a softball game and had Archie Moore sliding into home plate. Archie was training to fight Harold Johnson and had maybe a $100,000 fight at stake. So here was Archie sliding, giving his manager a heart attack. Softball was never soft enough for fight managers.

Joey's retired now and he has devoted his free time to much more serious things. He now sells chemicals to independent jobbers in New York, New Jersey and Pennsylvania; but he does much more than sell chemicals. Like I said, fans tend to remember the bad mistakes that a guy makes, but how many of them have read in the papers about what Joey's doing now? Let me explain. Joey and Rosalie have a son, Carmen, and he is retarded. When the best medical minds told them that the best place for Carmen was an institution they decided to fight back – Carmen stayed at home. The boy is eighteen now and attends the St. John of God School for the Retarded in Westville, New Jersey.

Because of Carmen and the people of that school, Joey has devoted most of his free time to the problem of retardation. He organizes dinners and raffles, but more than that he stages benefits for them all the time. When he was champ he fought a non-title fight and donated his entire share to the school. Because of Joey, Carmen is doing well. His intelligence will never get beyond a seven year olds, but he's doing better than the doctors ever thought he would and they say it's because of the love and affection that he gets. Carmen has even learned to imitate Jimmy Durante, Humphrey Bogart and Jimmy Cagney and he's pretty good, too.

Joey has become involved with the President's Council on Mental Health. He was also invited to Washington several years ago by Sargent Shriver so that he could talk about some of his ideas on mental retardation. He told them how Carmen had progressed through sports and how it was helping other kids as well; this led directly to the organization of the Special Olympics for the Retarded by Sargent Shriver. In one of the Special Olympic Games Carmen won five gold medals. In fact, the sister of Ted Kennedy, who is also retarded, pinned the gold medal on Carmen when he won the 50 yard dash.

Yes, Joey became a V.I.P., which is pretty good for a guy once called the "Bad Boy of Boxin'." In Philadelphia they call him "Pal Joey," boxing's pal and everybody else's.

ROUND 7

"The Uncrowned Champ"

Eastside, West side, all around the town they are saying Billy Graham won the fight, and they could be right, too. It certainly wasn't a popular decision. In my book, Graham should be the new welterweight champion

Joe Williams – New York
World Telegram—August, 1951

The Giardello-Graham bout in 1952 was unusual for several reasons, not the least of which was a helluva good fight. One judge had it seven to three for Billy, The other two officials had it five to four and one even and six to four for Joey. The six to four scorecard caused all the controversy. The six to four card showed that Joey had been awarded the tenth round while both other officials had that round for Billy. Commissioner Christenberry then took the tenth round into consideration and took a poll of the ringside writers. They were unanimously in favor of Graham, making it five to five even. This made Graham the winner.

Then Joey's manager took the decision before the Supreme Court, claiming that an official decision was changed by the commissioner.

The court voted in favor of Giardello, reversing the commissioner. Graham now had lost the same fight twice.

I think the only guys who took a beating were the bookmakers in this "I won, He won" free-for-all. In many of the bets they paid off on both guys as winners. I don't think Billy or Joey were really concerned at that point as to who won. They had a great fight, a big gate and the opportunity to fight each other again in the near future.

Billy Graham was born in New York City in 1921, and had never fought an A.A.U. amateur fight except for some bootleg fights out of town. In 1936 at fifteen, he signed for the Golden Gloves, but was rejected because of a heart murmur. In 1937, 1938, 1939, and in 1940 he was again rejected for the same reason. After the first two rejections he used assumed names but he still couldn't crack the New York *Daily News*, which sponsored the "Gloves." In 1940-his fifth try-he almost made it. He got past the *Daily News*, but was rejected a few minutes before fight time by the doctor. It turned out to be the same doctor that examined him the year before.

It's funny, but Billy got a lot of heat from his neighborhood crowd. They would razz him, saying, "What, rejected again?" Finally his dad took him to a heart specialist and learned that it was just an irregular heartbeat. Billy's heart was fine. Anyway, the whole thing seems funny when something like that is behind you and nothing serious ever came of it, but it can certainly bother you and even scare you at the time.

In my case I got a check-up in my training camp where I was getting ready for a fight in 1956 and they told me that my heart wasn't beating right. So I went over to Miami University, where I was examined by a prominent heart specialist. He told me that he had retired football players with what I had, an irregular heartbeat. I was really scared.

So when I went back and talked to my manager I went up to the Massachusetts General Hospital. I'll never forget it. I was there four days. They put me through a whole battery of tests, and I mean tests. After the three or four days they gave me a clean bill of health. They said my heart was naturally a little irregular but it didn't mean anything and I could do anything I wanted. But, of course, it set me back three months and we had to spend some money at the hospital. But I got a letter saying I was okay and the National Boxing Commission then let me box. Another incident with my heart was in 1970. I was watching TV when all of a sudden I got pains in my chest. I got up and walked around for a little, and eventually they went away. But as soon I sat down again the pains came back. I told my wife Gerri that I never had pains like this before, and so I called my doctor; naturally, he wasn't home. A few minutes later I got into my car and drove three miles to the veterans' hospital; it was the closest hospital. When I described the symptoms to the doctor he said that I'd had a slight coronary. Now, even I knew that meant my heart and I was scared. They hooked me up to a heart machine for three days and three nights. I never left that bed. All the time I was watching the heart machine ticking away like in a "Frankenstein" picture. By the fourth day the doctor said, "Willie, we can't find anything wrong with your heart." So they gave me a series of extensive tests and finally discovered that I had a hiatus Ulcer. So I went home and I've never had any trouble with it since. But there was something funny about it. The day before I left the hospital I was lying in bed and I turned on the radio and I hear Joe Garagiola burying me. He was saying that Willie Pep, one of the greatest fighters who ever lived, was broke and dying in a veterans hospital. Now I wasn't dying and I wasn't broke; the only reason I went to the V.A. hospital was that it was the closest. But Joe gave me one heck of an epitaph and a good laugh.

So in 1941, as a tall 126 pound featherweight, Billy Graham started his professional career at the age of twenty with an irregular heartbeat and no amateur fights. Irish Billy went on to win Fifty-eight fights in a row in the featherweight, lightweight and welterweight ranks. In fact, in 1942 we almost fought, but for one reason or another the fight never came off. Anyway, Tony Pellone broke Billy's win streak in a highly controversial decision. It was fought at the Queensboro arena in Long Island City in 1945. The first few rounds were fought in the rain, which slowed down the fast Graham, but he finished strong. Now, this was the year that the commission put in the "point" rule. A year later Billy came back to beat Tony in Madison Square Garden- Billy's first Friday night fight.

Retiring in 1955, Billy had 131 bouts, losing only 14. He had a lot of draws though- 15 of them. He had less than thirty fights from 1950-1955, yet these were his money years and his popularity grew as he fought such people as Gavilan, Giardello, Basilio, Aragon, Paddy Young,

Castellani, Vejar and Herring. As a light-welterweight he spotted lots of pounds to middleweights and still beat them.

He was a great boxer with good punching power to keep off the real strong ones like Giardello and Gavilan. He was an aggressive boxer and was an exceptional inside fighter and counter puncher.

Billy was no stranger to Kid Gavilan, they had fought each other four times. Billy beat the Kid in a ten rounder, but lost the second ten-round go in a split decision, and was "robbed" of the crown in their title fight. When the decision was announced, Madison Square Garden roared with 19,000 angry spectators; nobody could believe the decision. Billy, now at age thirty, had worked hard for ten years to reach that title fight and he was furious.

Gavilan started the fight strong and it took Billy a few rounds to get going. By the eleventh round it was an even fight. Then, in the last five rounds Billy came on strong and won at least four of them. He probably fought the greatest fight of his career against the Kid. He would jab and wait for Gavilan's lead. He would pick off the champ's left hook or slide inside his swinging right to the body. If Gavilan punched for the head, Billy rode with the blow. He had the better of the infighting. After it was all over, the Kid was exhausted from warding off Billy's savage attacks.

The referee judged it seven to seven, and one round even and gave the points' edge to Gavilan. One judge gave it to Graham and the second judge gave his vote to Gavilan.

All the ringside writers unanimously scored it in Billy's favor and called him the new champion of the world, although it's not that way in the record books. The thousands who witnessed this great bout all pointed to Graham as the winner and new champ. If there was ever a fight that the decision should have been reversed, this was it, and not the Giardello-Graham bout where no title was at stake.

Billy's only other championship bouts were with Carmen Basilio, for the New York State welterweight title. They fought twice for this title in 1953. The first one, won by Basilio, was so close that it prompted a rematch. The return was called a draw. They were both state champs.

Talking about Carmen, I first saw him back in 1949 in Syracuse when I boxed a Frenchman called Jean Mougin; they had Carmen on the six-round semifinal. I was very impressed with Carmen, his movements and his roughness; he never stopped walking in and finally knocked the guy out in two rounds. I thought then that this kid was one to be reckoned with; six years later he won the welterweight title. Carmen was always in top condition and trained harder than anybody I knew. Billy Backus, who won the welterweight title from Jose Napoles in 1970, is Carmen's nephew. Imagine, two champions in one family.

Like Billy Graham, Carmen was another of those Friday Heroes. He won the welterweight crown from Tony DeMarco in 1955 after Tony had taken it from Johnny Saxton that same year. After Basilio kayoed Tony in twelve rounds to win the title, he repeated his act in the exact same round in their rematch.

This guy from Canastota, New York, who worked the onion farms as a kid, lost his title to Johnny Saxton the following year in a questionable decision. However, in the return, that same year, Carmen fought the only way he could beat Saxton-he kayoed Johnny in nine rounds. Johnny, a two-time welterweight champ, fought Basilio again in 1957 and Carmen didn't waste any time. He stopped Saxton this time in two rounds. The following year Saxton quit the business.

That same year Carmen challenged and beat Sugar Ray Robinson for the middleweight title. Carmen, who traded a lot of punches in his fights, took a hell of a shellacking from Ray in the return, losing the crown. The big guys with the big bombs finally got to Carmen after his loss to Robinson. The "gutsy" Basilio was stopped twice by Gene Fullmer in middleweight title bouts- fourteen and twelve round kayoes.

After an exciting and profitable career, Carmen retired in 1961 after losing to Paul Pender, the middleweight champ who had knocked off Ray Robinson. Ray, who always seemed to be around, year after year, held the middleweight title on five different occasions.

Anyway, Billy Graham, the kid from New York's Hell's Kitchen, now lives with his family in Long Island. He's successfully employed as a sales representative for a large liquor company, a line he's been in since his retirement in 1955. When Irish Billy Graham is greeted today, it's always "Hi Champ." The public has not forgotten this guy and his fight with the "Kid" way back on August 29, 1951. They don't all forget, I guess.

ROUND 8

"THE BOLO KID"

BILLY GRAHAM'S REMATCH WITH GAVILAN was a year later in 1952 in Havana, the Kid's home town. As Billy tells it, "He beat me decisively in the fifteen-round title fight. "Yes, the kewpie-face Cuban kid made it unanimous against Billy, who was thirty-one by then, and that ended the famous Graham-Gavilan series of four fights.

The Kid, whose real name is Gerardo Gonzales, was born outside of Havana in 1926. As a little tot, he worked the sugarcane fields along with his family.

It was in the fields that the Kid developed his "bolo punch." It was the sweeping motion that field workers use with the "bolo knife" in cutting sugarcane.

As a brawling kid of the sugarcane fields, Gavilan made his way to Havana at the age of sixteen and started his amateur career. Within a year or so he was the most popular amateur in Havana and had acquired a new name, "Kid Gavilan" meaning "Kid Hawk."

He was touted by the Cubans as another Kid Chocolate, and in 1946 Kid Chocolate's old backers, who were still active in Havana at that time, financed Gavilan's campaign in the United States.

The Kid's road wasn't easy. By 1947 he had grown into the welterweight class, a division headed by Ray Robinson at the time. But the Cuban Kid was ready for anybody. Promoters would dig up the

roughest and toughest fighters for him. He never backed off and would challenge anyone from 135-165 pounds.

He impressed everyone in a losing effort with Ray Robinson and by beating Tony Pellone in 1948 and whipping Ike Williams twice in 1949. This work earned him a title shot against Sugar Ray in 1949. The Kid put on a great show but lost the fifteen rounder; however, in both defeats to Ray it was obvious that he was the number one contender and that if Sugar Ray vacated the Kid would be his successor.

It didn't take long until Gavilan became one of television's favorite performers, with his fancy footwork that resembled a rhumba routine and the sweeping bolo punch. Gavilan's bolo, in my opinion, didn't have much power; the Kid used it strictly for the fans. Of his 144 total bouts, he had only a 20 percent kayo ratio. The only guy I can remember who packed a big league wallop behind a bolo punch was the Philippines' Ceferino Garcia, a former middleweight champ in the thirties and early forties. Now, Garcia's bolo was dynamic and most of his many kayo victims got a taste of it. Though Ginks beat Garcia, he can verify his "bolo" power.

Robinson vacated his welterweight title in 1951 and, sure enough, the Kid beat Johnny Bratton for the title in the elimination tournament, although he wasn't recognized world-wide because Charley Humez of France and Billy Graham were strong challengers. Humez finally outgrew the 147 pound class and campaigned as a middleweight and Billy Graham lost the decision in 1951.

1953 was a winning year for the Kid. He deflated Chuck Davey who was very hot at the time and beat Carmen Basilio and Johnny Bratton in title bouts. Yet, the very next year was the beginning of the end for Gavilan. First, in April, he challenged middleweight champ Carl "Bobo" Olson for his crown at Chicago Stadium. The Kid went in at his heaviest, 155 pounds, and this added weight reduced his usual speed and made him a mark for the sharp-hitting Olson.

He was beaten without a doubt by the bigger and stronger Bobo, showing again that a welterweight champ rarely beats a middleweight champ. This happened to Carmen Basilio.

In the latter part of 1954, he lost a controversial decision and his title to Johnny Saxton. The Kid, who used to catch the judges' eyes with his spurts and flashes to get the nod in a close one, got a real bad decision. 98 percent of the ringside reporters had the Kid as the winner.

The colorless Saxton, who never won over the fans, didn't show any signs of championship form. It was more what the Kid did *not* do rather than what Saxton did. It was really "not a best effort" by Gavilan.

It was bold, but he had told millions of viewers after the fight on a TV interview that he expected to lose unless he scored a knockout. What he insinuated was that with Saxton's manager, Blinky Palermo, you had to kayo Johnny or lose. Blinky had a little something to say to Gavilan after that.

As for the Kid, his days as a top-notch fighter were over. He began to show weakness even before the Olson and Saxton fights. He fought Basilio and did manage a split decision after being floored. The Kid, down for a nine count, experienced his third knockdown of his career. A more aggressive Basilio could have ended it then and there, but he played it cautiously, too. The Kid, who loved to dance the rhumba and the mambo, was having good times together with his co-manager Angel Lopez, owner of New York's Chateau Madrid and one-time manager of Kid Chocolate in the thirties. He was keeping late hours before his fights. I think that his not being in shape for his fights was to be the biggest single factor in his fast decline.

As for the ex-champion in 1955, his losing streak started with Bobby Dykes, Eduarde Lausse and a few others. From 1956 to his retirement in 1958, the Kid had eighteen bouts; he won only six of them.

Gavilan was a good boxer, but not exceptional. He was fast, strong and could take a hell of a punch with his iron chin. In his two bouts with Sugar Ray, Robinson tried but couldn't put him down. But to keep going a long time in boxing you have got to be more than a good boxer. In addition, you can't be a catcher and the Kid caught quite a few.

Look, I fought more professional fights than anybody in modern boxing, 241 of them, totaling almost 2000 rounds. In my first six years I had almost two bouts a month, averaging over thirteen rounds a month. In the next six, the jabs and punches caught me a little more often and I had slightly over a bout a month. And for the last ten I was reduced to less than a bout a month. I was slowing down because I was getting older. But my point is that I only lasted as long as I did because I didn't take that many punches. I don't know much about baseball, but in boxing it's better to be a "pitcher" than a "catcher."

Let's say the average boxer takes twenty punches a round. Then the sub-average boxer or the slugger takes maybe thirty punches or jabs and the exceptional boxer, say, takes only ten. So the difference in either case is ten blows more or less. If we talk about 1000 career rounds the punch differential would be 10,000. Ouch!

This is why sluggers who can't box don't last long. An excellent boxer like Muhammad Ali will last longer than Joe Frazier. Jake LaMotta, one of the better middleweight champions, was one who would take four or five punches to get one good one in. The Bronx Bull had a little over 100 bouts in his twelve year career, but those tactics finally took the gas out of him. I guess there are boxing styles and people are built for just certain ones. You fight the only way you know how.

The late Bill Corum, the great sportswriter and sportscaster for the then New York *Journal American*, gave me a tag about my fighting style. I could never shake it. After one of my fights with Chalky Wright, he said I was elusive and quick and called me "Will o' the Wisp." Maybe it should have been "Will o' the Wop."

It was the end of the line for the "Bolo Kid." For a long time, he fought hard and was the best around. He created excitement with his famous "bolo punch," a punch which would begin at the floor and spiral upwards until it landed on or usually whizzed by the other guy's chin. He had a knack for showmanship that earned him thirty-four appearances on national television and had millions of viewers following his great career.

When boxing fans talk about the forties and fifties, the Kid's name is always mentioned along with his bolo punch. The Kid, who today is an athletic instructor for a boy's club in Miami, was a "fabulous" fighter.

ROUND 9

"THE LITTLE PROFESSOR"

Chuck Davey is a bright young man, and a holder of two degrees; Kipling
he has on the ropes, and Shakespeare on his knees,
But this wasn't Rudyard and this wasn't Bill,
This was The Hawk that swoops to kill
-and he learned about fighters from him.

Oh, Davey is fast and Davey is lean,
His right is fancy and his left is mean;

Vejar and Williams had to pay.
But this wasn't the Chico and this wasn't Ike.
This was The Kid from Camaguey
-and he learned about fighters from him.

On Michigan State's Classic halls,
The ivy rustles on the walls;
And a boy who wishes to take up dancing,
Needs go no farther than old East Lansing.
But unless, as a fighter, he's going to meet schmoes,
-the school to attend is Sloppy Joes

Bill Corum- New York
Journal - American - 1953

I WAS ON MY THIRD CUP of coffee and second donut when Johnny the Greek, who owns the Plaza Diner, walked over. Naturally, we are all talking then about boxing and so Johnny, who is not a big fight fan, joins in the conversation by asking about a boxer. "Whatever happened to Chuck Davey?"

Now, that just goes to show you what television did for boxing. I mean, here's a guy who isn't a big fight fan and yet he can remember the name of a guy who only fought for a short time, twenty years ago. Chuck Davey! That son-of-a-gun must have been the all-time champion for being popular on TV. Davey, he was a natural for TV, a handsome blonde Irish kid, and college graduate, who could knock out the ladies even faster than his opponents. He'd throw about a thousand punches a fight. There was constant action. He took good and he got promoted to TV. In a matter of a few fights he was at the top and in constant demand. Of course, he eventually ran into the "Gay Cabellero, "Kid Gavilan, much too soon, and it was a disaster. But that's a long story.

Chuck was born in Detroit in 1925 and learned to box early. He entered a boxing school when he was twelve and there he learned to box. But as a kid, boxing wasn't the main thing. Through his mother's urging and influence, his education became the center of his life. However, when he enrolled at Michigan State University he naturally went out for the boxing team. There he became the N.C.A.A. Featherweight Champion in 1943.

But like most of us at the time, everything had to wait for the war, and Chuck spent three years in the Air Force as a navigator. He got out around 1945 and went back to Michigan State University. Back in school he was named captain of the boxing team, and in 1948 he got to be N.C.A.A. Champion again. In that same year he beat Johnny Saxton in the semifinals of the Olympic trials. Then in 1949 he grew to a welterweight and won that N.C.A.A. title. He graduated with a Bachelor of Science degree in 1949 and an amateur record of ninety-three wins in ninety-four bouts. He was also the only man to win four N.C.A.A. titles. Now Chuck really liked to fight; which was something unusual for a college graduate; so he figured he could turn pro and make enough money to continue his education. He turned professional and in 1951 he got his masters' degree in education and a job as a teacher in a junior high school. He was fighting and going to school.

Chuck had seen a lot of guys make a good deal of money in a very short time. He had a good record going for him, plus, he knew he was colorful; so Chuck figured he could make it. In addition, he thought his education taught him quick thinking, which is a great asset to a boxer. I personally don't know about college helping you to be quick of mind. We had plenty of real good fighters who were quick of mind but never even went to high school. I'm not saying that going to college hurts you as a fighter. Billy Soose, a tough middleweight champion who later went on into the heavyweight division, graduated from Penn State and in some ways was similar to Chuck Davey. Soose started his professional career in 1938 and by 1941, only three years later, beat Ken Overlin for the middleweight title. Soose in his fast rise fought the best in his class- Tami Mauriello, Tony Zale and Georgie Abrams. Soose was unbeaten as a middleweight champ, vacated his title and went on to campaign as a light-heavyweight. Only after a couple of fights in that division he was drafted into the Navy and never returned to the ring.

College doesn't help once you climb in the ring. It may help when it comes to cutting up the purses with your manager, but once you get in the ring all the college you've got isn't going to help you. You've got to know how to box, you've got to be in shape and you've got to have the will to win.

Myself, I never went beyond high school. In Hartford, Connecticut, I was a very ordinary student. I didn't like school much and I liked it even less when I started fighting amateur in my junior year. From then on I kind of majored in truancy. But before I went into fighting full time, I finished my four years. I liked all the other sports in high school but I was only 105 pounds, which was too small for football or basketball. However, I did play shortstop on the baseball team - good field, no hit. But really boxing was my thing since I was fifteen and a half years old.

At one point Davey, too, quit school (teaching) and became a full-time fighter. By the end of 1951 he had won thirty-seven out of thirty-nine with two draws, one which was with Carmen Basilio, and the other with a guy named Ross Virgo. Chuck had the record and he had the looks. And he had that thing called style. Davey was a southpaw, and with all that speed he could thoroughly confuse a slower opponent. All he really needed was a break and the right promotion. But his people would have to pick his opponents carefully to get him to the top, because he couldn't hit hard, and a good, experienced ranking welterweight with a lot of speed might hurt him.

Well, television did it for him. In January of 1952 he got about $800 for an eight rounder in Chicago, and he looked good. So they set him up right away with Ike Wiliams, who had been the lightweight champion and had 150 fights and had a terrific punch. Now, old Ike knew his business and he could punch, but he was slowing down and Chuck was very fast, and very smart. This was Davey's first television fight. As expected, Chuck, with that lightning speed, hit Ike constantly round after round. Davey looked great and piled up the points. Now when you get hit that many times it's got to hurt you, eventually. Finally, it got to Williams and he was through. Chuck caught him with a left to the body that sent him into the ropes and as he came off the ropes Chuck caught him again and sent him back into the ropes. There the referee stopped it. It was the fifth round. After the bout, Blinky Palermo, who managed Ike, made one of his predictions: This kid Davey is great- he's really going places."

Chuck Davey was on his way. He got $4000 for that fight. Shortly after that he fought Chico Vejar on national TV and won a ten-round decision. For that work, he got about $6000. Then after a draw with tough Carmen Basilio, Chuck came right back to beat Chico again. It was on national TV again, only this time he stopped him in five rounds and picked up $11,000. Next he went back in against Carmen Basilio and this time he won a disputed ten-round decision. But it was a win, and in September of 1952 he fought ex-champ Rocky Graziano on national TV and he out speeds him and out-boxes him and gets the ten-round decision and $16,000. That was Rocky's last; he announced his retirement after the fight.

Television found its fair-haired boy of the Friday Night Fights. Though he fought popular, well known but slower opponents, he still out-boxed them and beat them. The public loved it. He picked up around forty grand in those nine months; he became a household word; and they started talking about a championship shot with Kid Gavilan. Well, you can't blame Chuck Davey. He'd beaten everybody they put him in with, including some big names. He was a good, fast, clever southpaw boxer. Chuck was also getting what he wanted. He was making money fast and he was near the top. Now maybe if his people were thinking in terms of a long career they would have slowed him down a little and gradually worked his way up in the rankings. I mean there were an awful lot of talented guys around at the time like Johnny Saxton, Bobby Dykes, Johnny Bratton, Billy Graham and Gil Turner. They all deserved a shot at Gavilan's title. Now maybe Davey could have beaten them, but he hadn't was the point. And they all were mostly faster than the guys he had been fighting, and they could punch as well as box. Who knows? Anyway, his people weren't taking any chances. Also the promoters knew that he was a hero overnight, that the television fans loved him and they thought him invincible. At that point they just couldn't take a chance on having him lose what with a rich Gavilan fight just around the corner.

While they were setting up a Gavilan fight, they went looking for opponents for Davey. He was supposed to fight Del Flanagan but he backed out saying that the styles were too similar and it wouldn't make for a good fight. Who knows who said what to whom in the back room. I mean they didn't want him losing so maybe they were being simply over cautious. But if he was going to fight Gavilan for the championship of the world he should have had no trouble with Del Flanagan. But he got bad press because of it. It wasn't his fault. The promoters were just as interested in seeing him continue to win before a fight with the Kid.

Instead of Del Flanagan, in December, 1952 they matched him with Fritzie Pruden, a hard-hitting welterweight from Canada and that fight turned out to be very interesting. Chuck won it on a third round TKO, but most people felt the referee stopped it too quickly. People began to think that maybe they were protecting Davey. But what they didn't realize, or forgot, was that just a few years earlier in the same ring Ray Robinson caught Jimmy Doyle with a left hook and the guy died. This had to be on the referee's mind. And besides, Chuck was beating the guy. He had Fritzies mouthpiece out and had put him down and he was all over him. Chuck had made about $50,000 that year, and he had started off with an $800 bout.

The next month Chuck fought an unranked guy by the name of Johnny Williams in a tune-up for Gavilan. It wasn't much of a fight, but it gave him a workout, like punching a bag, and he got the chance to promote the Gavilan fight a little more by showing what he could do. Davey would back up and jab, jab and annoy the hell out of the guy. He could back up and move away so fast that almost everybody missed him. He was lightning with his feet, like Sugar Ray, and he still had enough zing in his jab so that he could hurt you going away. But at the same time he could stop, come down flat-footed, and bang away with his left. And being a southpaw this was always "backwards" to his opponent, and it would startle the hell out of him.

Then he fought Williams and they kept track for a while of how many times he hit him. Davey caught him 97 times in the third round and 111 times in the fourth. 111 times! That's about two shots every three seconds. It was ridiculous. Chuck wore him down and then knocked him out in the seventh round.

That set up the big fight, which was equally ridiculous, but the other way around. It was in February 1953. People were reading about it all over the world. Television had brought it about and millions and millions of people watched it on TV, but it was an awful show. Davey was their hero; he had beaten Rocky Graziano and Carmen Basilio. The guy had looked great on TV. Yet, people, new fight fans, never thought about the fact that he had never fought a top ten ranking welterweight contender and those guys he did fight were out of their prime. And so he was still really more or less unranked, yet here he was going against the champion of the world.

For the first two rounds the Kid didn't do anything. He just kind of sized up Davey. But in the third he came out firing with both hands and caught him with a right to the head, and down went Chuck Davey for the count of nine. Now Davey hadn't ever been down before; he was beginning to see the difference between a professional and an amateur. Then it started to get ridiculous. The Kid figured it would be fun to teach Chuck how to box, so he turns around and fights him southpaw. Davey's jabs now weren't doing anything but the "Keed," even though he's backwards, southpaw, is doing great. He was doing Davey's thing. He kept that up from the fourth through the sixth, beating Davey left-handed. The "hero" began to look tarnished. But heroes don't fall that easily. Davey had lots of guts; he wouldn't have been in there in the first place otherwise. He showed a lot of durability, taking Gavilan's best shots for eight rounds. But it was just a matter of time. Chuck charged out for the ninth round figuring he had to knock out Gavilan to win and he was doing pretty good until the Kid countered with his right and Chuck was down. He got up but Gavilan caught him with two more real bombs and Davey was down two more times. The referee waived "three knockdown rule," plus the bell, saved him, but it was over.

Davey's handlers, who had probably taken chances with other guys before, wouldn't this time. Chuck wanted to go out for the tenth round, but his trainer, Issy Kline, stood in front of Chuck when the bell rang for the tenth and wouldn't let him come out. Davey was hurt bad; it was the right thing to do.

So that was it. No more hero. Television had created Chuck Davey and when it was finished with him, it dropped him. I suppose the guy could have backed up, started all over again, and come along slow like he should have in the first place. But there wasn't any point to it. As a TV hero he could never be the same. Maybe he could have gotten better. But the letdown must have been a shock to him. Besides he had done what he set out to do. He made a lot of money in a hurry. He got about $45,000 for the Gavilan title bout.

Of course, Chuck loved the sport and he hung around for a while. He knocked out Sammy Guiliani right after the Gavilan bout and then went on to lose-two straight to Al Andrews. Then he lost to Art Aragon in Los Angeles, and finally was knocked out by Vince Martinez in 1954. At that point he retired. All this time he had a television sport show in Detroit, because of his popularity, and that added a few dollars to his bank account.

After being out of the ring for about a year, he decided to come back. However, after two fights winning both of them, he retired for good.

He only had one great year of fame and fortune, but he got out with his own home, cash in the bank and a masters' degree from Michigan State University. That's a future. He's since gone on to build up a lucrative insurance business in Detroit and become the boxing commissioner of the state of Michigan. The commission belongs in the hands of fighters and not the politicians.

In Connecticut, we have a woman commissioner. We have a position called Commissioner of Consumer Protection, and part of that job is being boxing commissioner. Now what does she know about boxing? Not that it's her fault, but this is the way it is almost everywhere- the commissioner is a political appointee and who gets the job depends on being in the right party at the right time.

So you get a lot of weird things happening with commissioners who don't understand boxing. Sometimes it's just bad rulings. Other times you get terrible mismatches that can and have resulted in boxers getting seriously hurt in the ring. That doesn't do the sport any good. In fact, right after the Clay-Liston championship fight in Lewiston, Maine, in 1965, Connecticut banned boxing on the grounds that it's too bloody. Yet, that fight for the heavyweight championship wasn't really bloody, even though Liston was stopped in a strange first round.

Boxing doesn't have any more injuries or fatalities than sports like football or hockey. But what they did in Connecticut was to deprive the kids of the game for seven years. Instead of pulling kids in off the streets and teaching them discipline and physical fitness, you've got them out there killing themselves with drugs.

Connecticut was always a big boxing state. Just in the featherweight class you had three world champions. Louis "Kid" Kaplan, "Battling" Battalino and myself. But thanks to the efforts of a few people like State Senator Joe Felicio, who came out of a tough neighborhood and knows what it is for a kid to take up boxing, the sport is coming back to Connecticut.

But we still have a woman commissioner. What they should do is appoint men who really know the game, who contributed a lot to the Sport in Connecticut and who really are interested in helping to promote boxing. Some years back we had an ex-boxer, Denny McMahon, as a commissioner and he did a wonderful job until he retired.

Chuck Davey got to be commissioner and that's great in my book. And, not the least of all, guys like Johnny the Greek still remember him. Twenty years go by and a guy like Johnny, over some coffee, remembers one of Friday's Heroes.

"THE TAILOR IN SECAUCUS"

AFTER WE LEFT THE PLAZA DINER we walked across Patterson Plank road to Al Certo's Custom Tailor Shop. I've known Al for quite a while and I have all my clothes made at his shop, since he opened four years ago. He has tailors from the old country working for him and they can really give you a fit. Lots of show business customers buy there, like Jack Kelly, Jimmy Roselli, Joey Adams and Mike Mazaurki, plus most of the ex-boxers from Jack Dempsey on down. Yeah, Al makes great clothes.

I've always been hooked by good-looking clothes and I spent a lot of money on wardrobes during my lifetime. I guess being champ you also had to look like one. But anyway, there were two suits that really paid off for me.

From 1940-1943 I won sixty-two in a row. Around my seventh or eighth fight I bought a new suit. I bought it the day of the fight and that night I won my fight. So every fight night I wore that suit, through sixty-two fights. There was a good friend of mine, Charley Green, "Shyki," we used to call him. Now, Shyki would come down to all my fights. On my sixty-third fight, when I got licked by Sammy Angott, I took off my suit that night and I said, "Shyki," I'm giving you a brand new suit. I only wore it fifty to fifty-five times." He was my size, so he took the suit. I then went out and bought another lucky suit. I wore it strictly on fight night. Sure enough, Shyki would be around like a vulture, figuring that as soon as I lose the fight he would wind up with another suit. But he had to wait for another seventy-three fights. The seventy-fourth fight was the Saddler fight and I lost. So after a period of six years and seventy-four fights I said, "Shyki, here's another suit, though it is a little older than the other one."

Anyway, Al Certo was an ex-boxer himself; he was the 135 pound Golden Gloves Champ and ran a professional streak of twenty straight wins, eleven by kayoes, before an accident in his brother's car wash station ended his career. But Al has always stayed close to boxing and kids' physical fitness programs. He's staged several hundred benefit boxing cards using former great fighters and local amateurs to raise money for the Police Athletic League programs, Cerebral Palsy, and for a lot of down-and out boxers.

Al, as head of the Secaucus Police Athletic League, stages weekly boxing matches among kids from the ages of eight through fifteen. At forty-five this guy with a heart of gold is planning to build a sports center for kids. Naturally, boxing will have a high priority when this center becomes a reality.

Anyway, Al always helps out when he can, and this Christmas he was going all out. He's agreed to make the fairy-tale costumes for Chico from some of his left over stuff. There would be elf costumes and a couple of clown costumes.

The plan was for us guys to dress up at Al's shop and drive with the costomes on to Newark Airport and meet the other guys. Al wouldn't be able to come because of the Christmas rush in finishing customers' suits.

Ernie Durando and Tippy Larkin had arrived and we were still waiting for Charley Fusari. Ernie and Tippy, both quiet guys, were pacing up and down the showroom with their clown costumes on and occasionally looking up at the framed photographs of celebrities Al had hanging on the walls.

Ernie, at age forty-seven, is over his old fighting weight but still looks like the slick kayo artist of the early fifties. The "Rock," as he was called, had his last bout in 1957 when he lost a decision to champion Gene Fullmer in a non-title fight. This was Gene's tune-up prior to the rematch with Ray Robinson who he had beaten earlier for the middleweight title.

Ernie, who won more than half of his fifty pro fights by knockouts, fought some of the best 160 pound wars of the late forties and early fifties. He had three great fights with Rocky Castellani, losing two decisions and kayoing Rocky in the third. In this bout Rocky's manager, was suspended from boxing after having his own private fight with the referee, who had stopped the bout in favor of Durando.

The big rivalry Ernie had was against Paddy Young. They had five fights that were equivalent to twenty fights of today. I think they both used each other up in these rough and tough fights and may have shortened their careers. Of the five fights, Ernie won one, lost three decisions and drew one. Paddy was a real tough guy and looked it, too. Paddy, like Ernie, was a puncher, the kind that could belt you out with one shot. He loved to box the guys who walked into him so he could catch them cold. He had his worst troubles with the classic boxers; the left jab always bothered him. They were both sluggers who stood toe to toe and fought it out, and that's why the Durando-Young fights were so great. When these two guys were fighting they packed Madison Square Garden. Paddy from Greenwich Village section of New York City and Ernie from Bayonne, New Jersey, had their followers coming out in droves and the promoters loved every money minute of it. In addition to the big live gates, there was television to boot.

Like Ernie, Paddy fought the best around in his prime, like Gavilan, Graham, Dauthville, Fusari. In the Bobo Olson fight, in the eliminations for the middleweight championship of the world, Bobo cut Paddy to pieces with his left jab. Bobo was a very good boxer.

For the last sixteen years Ernie has been working for the New Jersey Turnpike Authority as a safety coordinator, inspecting construction projects on the turnpike. Ernie, unlike Rodney Dangerfield, gets a lot of respect.

Tippy Larkin, who at fifty-five doesn't look his age, was looking at some of the haberdashery, shirts and ties and checking the price tags to kill time. He looked kind of cute in his clown's costume. Tippy, always reserved and unassuming, was one of the great welterweights of the late thirties and forties and won the junior welterweight title in

1946 from Willie Joyce. Earlier he had lost his bid for the lightweight title against Beau Jack.

Tippy was the only guy ever to shut-out Freddie "Red" Cochrane. He beat him five straight. After Cochrane became welterweight champion Tippy couldn't get a fight with Red and make it six in a row. Of his 157 fights, Tippy lost 13 and fought the best- Henry Armstrong, Jackie "Kid" Berg and Lou Jenkins, just to name a few. This masterful boxer had nineteen main events at Madison Square Garden and earned over one million dollars during his eighteen year career. Retiring in 1953, Tippy is now a highway construction supervisor for a construction company in New Jersey.

It was getting pretty late and we still had a little drive to the airport when Charley Fusari walked in as if we had all the time in the world. That's Charley – calm and cool. That was the way he approached all of his fights, calm and cool. Charley was known as the "Fighting Milkman" with the "Milkman's Punch." He got this tag because he was delivering milk with his brother in Irvington, New Jersey, before and during his early pro career. His brother would drive the truck and Charley would scamper up and down the streets delivering the milk to the door - it kept him in shape.

He got a tough break in 1949 when he fought Rocky Graziano at the Polo Grounds. At that time, Charley was considered a great prospect for the welterweight title and had the ex-champ ragged for nine rounds. He gave Rocky a boxing lesson like he never had seen. But in the tenth round Rocky, with his "killer instinct," let loose with everything he had. He pinned Charley against the ropes, savagely clubbing him, holding him, clubbing him. The screaming crowd of about 40,000 went crazy-some were rooting for Rocky to finish it, and the others for Charley to hold on.

WITH ONLY FIFTY-SIX SECONDS TO GO referee Ruby Goldstein stopped the fight and Graziano won. According to Charley, who was 13 $^{1/2}$ pounds lighter than Rocky, he couldn't understand referee Ruby Goldstein's decision to stop it. First, he felt that Rocky should have been disqualified for grabbing his throat and choking him while belting him with his free hand. Secondly, he says he wasn't hurt at all from Rocky's punches.

This bout cost Charley a quarter of a million dollars in contracts already signed for boxing exhibitions throughout the United States. The contracts were only good if he beat Rocky. Charley was a popular boxer but mostly on the East Coast and he was to be showcased all over.

Rocky was in such a rage that he continued to pound Charley after the referee called a halt to the fight. Rocky was determined to win, and he did. This was the same kind of instinct that won him the title a few years earlier from Tony Zale.

Charley, after a good ring career which ended in 1953, is pretty well off from his ring earnings and is now a public relations man with a New Jersey wholesale liquor company.

Anyway, Charley hustled into his clown outfit and we were on our way to Newark Airport. Tippy, Ernie and Charley as clowns- Tiger, Ginks and me dressed up as elves.

ROUND 11

"CHICO"

SECAUCUS IS ONLY A STONE'S THROW from Newark, and we were at the airport in no time. I parked in the lot for short term parking and we piled out and headed for the waiting room of the terminal. Chico Vejar was standing near the doorway dressed up as Santa Claus.

How this guy Chico would organize this involved trip was unbelievable, but he had put it all together and here we were as one fighting team on Christmas Eve, ready to board the Executive jet for Appalachia.

I had never met Chico personally during his fighting days. I only got to know him in 1963 when he had called me for a charity appearance in Westchester County. This was about two years after his retirement from the ring.

Chico was another real TV idol. In fact, he ranks right behind Tiger Jones and Kid Gavilan with twenty-eight national appearances. But I guess his most dramatic television appearance was his last in 1961. It was a ten rounder at New York's St. Nick's Arena against Canada's Wilfie Greaves. Now Wilfie was former Canadian middleweight champ who was tough, but Chico beat Greaves in a unanimous decision. When the decision was announced, Chico asked Johnnie Addie, the announcer, for the microphone and stood in the center of the ring and announced his retirement, in a sort of farewell address to boxing.

That's the kind of class the guy has. I had never seen anything like this before in my life; I had never heard of a boxer doing that before. He paid his respects to the sport and to his loyal fans for their support throughout his twelve years as a professional. The speech was brief and to the point, and Chico left the ring with the cheers of the audience ringing in his ears. Chico Vejar was twenty-nine then and had fought 117 pro fights, winning 93 and losing 20, with 4 draws; yet a bigger fight loomed in his life.

Chico was of Chilean and Italian parents and was born in 1931 in Stamford, Connecticut. He was a high school dropout when he started fighting amateur in 1948 around the Connecticut area. He started using a phony name so his father wouldn't know he was boxing and ended up fighting his entire amateur career under the name of Chico Avalos. (It was the first name that came to his mind. A very good friend of his father's from Chile was named Avalos.) However, his father finally caught on because Chico couldn't hide his bruises. His father didn't like it much, but boxing gave Chico the discipline he needed. He went back to high school and graduated.

In 1949, at New York City's Sunnyside Gardens, Chico was fighting a tough amateur when he caught the eye of the late Steve Ellis, a popular and well-known radio and television commentator. Steve was very promotional minded and had Chico train at the 17th Street CYO gym with trainers like Charley Goldman. Ellis applied all of his techniques, and made him popular within the course of a few months after turning professional in 1950.

He got more publicity than most veteran boxers could get with Steve's press connections. Before he met Steve, Chico had only one pair of trunks. Steve took Chico to Everlast, the company that makes boxing equipment, and outfitted him with three or four pairs of everything a boxer needs. Chico continued to mix fighting and schooling and in 1951 Chico started studying business administration and drama as a freshman student at New York University. Steve took care of Chico's transportation as he commuted to school from Stamford to New York. He was called "Stamford's Socking Schoolboy." By then he had won thirty-six of his first thirty-seven professional fights.

Chico fought his first main bout at Madison Square Garden against Eddie Compo and lost a split decision. His second at the Garden was with tough Enrique Bolanos, It was a TV fight and a real barnburner. Chico not only won the decision, but the hearts of fight fans across the nation. He became a symbol, the "nice kid fighting his way through college."

Chico fought on national television three times in fifty days at New York's Madison Square Garden, which was a shade behind Beau Jack's record of three in forty-eight days. His winning ways continued and his popularity with the TV viewers set the stage for the big blown-up fight with Chuck Davey. A four to one favorite, Chico hit the deck four times before losing a lopsided decision. It was the same story the second time they fought.

Everybody thought Chico had gone into the tank; they were sure he threw the fights. That's ridiculous, of course; Chico didn't throw those fights, and he was simply beaten. Chico had stretched his strength as he'd put it. He was attending school, working in the gym and appearing on shows. Probably this had something to do with him looking bad against Chuck Davey.

Chico learned how it was to be a loser, and after the Davey fights was drafted into the U.S. Army, where he served for two years. He made his comeback after his Army hitch with successive wins over Billy Graham and Vince Martinez, who was touted as the next middleweight champ. In addition, he fought Gene Fullmer, Joey Giardello, Art Aragon, Kid Gavilan and Joey Giambra.

He utilized his drama experience at New York University and landed a few movie parts in pictures with Tony Curtis (*The Midnight Story*) and two with the late Audio Murphy (*Three Guns West* and *World in my Corner*). In *World in my Corner* he played a champion boxer who mixes it up with Murphy. According to Chico, Audie could really handle his dukes.

The big day for Chico came in 1958 when his little boy Jimmy was born. Chico and his wife Caryl, married in 1956, named the baby after Caryl's doctor-father, James Damian, Damian being the patron saint of physicians. Life was happy in the Vejar home in Stamford, a two-family house Chico had bought with his ring earnings; his mother and father lived upstairs. Jimmy became the center of attention and Chico could talk for hours about him. When he was one year old, Chico began to notice that he wasn't developing as fast as other kids his age. Jimmy was having trouble with his coordination.

 112

As the months passed, Chico and Caryl finally determined that something was seriously wrong. The doctor's examination revealed that Jimmy had Cerebral Palsy.

You can imagine how this crushed Chico and Caryl. And they were scared for the future, Caryl was carrying their second child at the time. Lisa, now thirteen, and a second daughter, Rachel Damian, now eight, are the picture of health. No fist ever slammed into Chico's body like the doctor's words. His world seemed to collapse around him.

Chico made sure that Jimmy's precious last days were pleasant ones. He stayed by his son's side night and day. He played Jimmy's games, games of sound. It was the little boy's only way of communicating. Chico would hit a spoon on a pan and it delighted the boy. It was music to him. In his own little way, Jimmy was happy.

There were big medical bills to pay, so Chico continued fighting, but his twelve-year career was slowly coming to an end. It was during this period that Chico first got to know about the United Cerebral Palsy Fund.

The people from the Cerebral Palsy organization told him that they would help him with little Jimmy with their clinics and trained specialists. These people really wanted to help and they didn't ask for anything. Chico was so impressed that he joined them in the fight against Cerebral Palsy.

Chico plunged into volunteer projects, devoting much of his time to a fund-raising telethon. During the preparation of the nationwide telethon, he met David Osterer, president of the United Cerebral Palsy Association of Westchester County.

Like many others, Osterer was impressed with the passion of this ex-fighter who was working day and night to promote the C.P. telethon. They worked side by side and got to know each other during the months of preparation. The downhill fighter and Osterer, a wealthy industrialist and humanitarian, developed a strong friendship over their common cause.

It was arranged that Chico would appear on the television telethon with his son. The city of Stanford earlier had proclaimed a "Jimmy Vejar Day" and everyone was looking forward to the telethon. It was expected to be the biggest year for donations and the C.P. people needed the donations badly.

On the day of the telethon, Chico left for the Westchester unit of the telethon at the County Center in White Plains, New York. He was driving along the Cross Westchester Expressway from Stamford, when he heard over the radio that comedian Ernie Kovacs had been killed in an automobile accident. Now he didn't know Kovacs personally, but the news seemed to shock Chico. In the meantime at the C.P. unit, Osterer received a tearful call from Caryl.

Jimmy was dead.

For Osterer the most difficult thing he ever had to do was to break the news to Chico.

Chico took it like a champ. He went home to comfort his wife and made the arrangements for Jimmy's burial.

But this wasn't going to make him quit. He returned the next day and went before the cameras. No one knew about little Jimmy's death in the studio, not even Dennis James, the C.P. master of ceremonies –until Chico announced it to thousands of stunned viewers. Chico's first words were, "Jimmy couldn't be here today as we promised. He died yesterday."

Chico made a beautiful plea to the viewers and studio audience. Within fifteen minutes following Chico's ten-minute appearance, calls poured into the station. Officials estimated that Chico's appearance brought an additional $50,000 in pledges towards C.P.

Chico has been with United Cerebral Palsy ever since. (His boxing career had ended nine months before the telethon, when he beat Greaves at Old St. Nick's.) He brings the word to the people like a disciple through the many events he attends and stages. Everyone wants to hear Chico's story. They know what he says comes right from this heart.

Chico doesn't limit himself to C.P., but works for several charitable organizations. He recently sparked various fund-raising drives for New Horizons, an organization for the handicapped. In fact, that's how come we were all here at Newark Airport today. Chico learned of the plight of some children in a welfare hospital in the heart of the poverty-stricken Appalachia region. The hospital was poor, almost as poor as the families that had their children there.

Chico decided that they would have a Christmas they would always remember. He got to some people. He begged for toys and clothing from department stores. He begged for candy from candy manufacturers. And he got it all, including the use of the Executive Jet that we were to board soon. Everybody had opened their hearts and their pocketbooks for the kids and families in the poverty-stricken hospital. Chico made it happen.

He now needed helpers and as usual he called on some of the greatest guys in the world-the boxers. All athletes do a good job when it comes to charity, but fighters, I think, are the greatest. They never get paid a cent for their work and appearances and they pay their own expenses. The fight game is always there when people are in trouble.

At many benefits we put on boxing exhibitions. Joey Giardello put a big one together a few years ago in Philadelphia for the benefit of mentally retarded kids. It was a great show for the people. 4000 or more of them were there to see guys like Graziano, Fusari, Davey, Larkin, Basilio and Saddler. There were sixteen famous ex-fighters and eight of them former champions.

The spectators loved it. We would pelt and paw each other with huge 16 ounce gloves in eight three-round exhibitions. A lot of the guys were creaky-jointed, pot bellied and short-winded, but nevertheless performed with all the desire of the past.

That night Joey Giardello renewed his old rivalry with Billy Graham, and with his handsome teen-age kids as handlers, Chuck Davey faced Chico. As Chico and Chuck came out for the first round, a voice in the crowd yelled to Chico to "get even, get even."

Old Jake LaMotta squared off with Rocky Graziano and Rocky would pretend to get mad, half falling down punching at him, Rocky Castellani with Ernie Durando, Dan Bucceroni and Charley Norkus, Carmen Basilio and Tiger Jones, Tony Janiro and Charley Fusari, Tippy Larkin and Freddie Russo, and me with my old friend Sandy Saddler. I don't try to show him up in an exhibition. With a guy like Sandy you don't fool around because he's a very serious guy and keeps in shape.

There's a lot of comedy bits the guys do during their exhibitions-like taking pot shots at the referee and chasing him out of the ring. The guy I fool with at exhibitions is Freddie Russo, an ex-lightweight who had a great professional record. Of his 145 professional bouts he lost only 14. At one point he ran a string of 51 consecutive pro wins - a pretty tough task by anyone's standards.

I remember in 1951, while Freddie was making a comeback against Del Flanagan in St. Paul. Freddie had beaten Del's brother,

Glen, in a close ten rounder five years earlier and now matched with his younger brother Del. I happened to be there because my manager, Lou Viscusi, handled the Flanagan Brothers. I told Freddie that he was going to be in for a hell of a tough go against Del and Del proceeded to pitch a ten round shutout. After the bout, I drove Freddie back to his hotel and going over the bridge I asked him how he felt. He said, "Stop the car and I'll show you. "He got out of the car and dropped all his boxing gear off of the bridge that goes over the Mississippi. That was his last bout.

Freddie never fought me professionally, although he wishes he had. He would have given me a hell of a fight. Anyway, this bundle of energy wears a toupee and keeps it on when he boxes exhibitions. So when we box each other my finale is to spin him around like a top, snatch his toupee off, and place it on the referee's head.

Sometimes charity exhibitions get a bit serious. One time waiting to go in the ring with Freddie Russo, two guys got in the ring wearing gloves and all. They weren't boxers, they were businessmen around fifty years old. What had happened was that some guy promised to put up $1000 towards the charity if these two guys would face each other in the ring. It started pretty calm. Then one guy gets tagged on the nose and he goes wild. He tears into his opponent slamming away like a crazy man. He hit so hard that the other guy was carried out of the ring after being knocked down a couple of times. The guy's bridge was broken and bleeding. The guy who put up the $1000 really got his money's worth. Maybe he didn't like either one of them.

Chico, like Giardello, has staged hundreds of boxing benefits over the past ten years, and, believe me, it takes a lot of work. But Chico has found contentment. After twelve years of glorifying Chico Vejar, he is now glorifying other people.

He has the love of his daughters and his wife. They don't complain when he is called for benefit after benefit or maybe to address a civic and social for Cerebral Palsy. They know it is something he wants to do, for the member of the family who is no longer there.

ROUND 12

"THE TIMID TIGER"

THERE'S A TENDENCY FOR MOST PEOPLE to get kind of quiet on a plane. I guess because it's a little scary if you don't do it a lot. You get a little nervous and think about all kinds of crazy things. At least I do. Anyway, here we were, a bunch of guys dressed up ridiculously and I couldn't help but think that we looked awful small and silly up in the sky. Course, we all were kind of little, come to think to it. It's a funny thing, but today nobody pays much attention to the little guys in the ring. The heavyweights have the whole business wrapped up. In our day things were more in proportion. Of course, heavyweights have always been popular and there were plenty of great ones back then, too.

I guess just about everybody would think of Joe Louis first. Everybody knows his story about how he grew up as a poor, uneducated southern farm boy to become one of the greatest champs ever. And everybody knows about his great fights with all of the top heavies and light-heavies of the late thirties and forties; guys like Baer and Schmelling and Billy Conn, and how poor old Joe had to keep fighting till he was almost forty cause of his troubles with the tax people. People remember him for being a quiet kind-hearted fellow who was always a gentleman outside the ring. Joe was always offered as an example for American youth. Not just black American youth, but American youth. That's something that you see in sports today, but you didn't thirty-five years ago. In fact, Jackie Robinson used to say that Joe Louis' career had a lot to do with his being able to break the baseball color barrier with the Brooklyn Dodgers in 1947. At least it made it easier for him once he got there. But Joe Louis wasn't the first. There's a long line of black champions going all the way back to Jack Johnson; too many, in fact, to name. A few that come to mind though were Henry Armstrong, Joe Gans, Tiger Flowers, Ray Robinson, and Chalky Wright. And there have been champions of every race and creed from every continent. You've got to give boxing its credit for that. Joe Louis is just one example of what it's offered a lot of guys.

Like I said, there were a lot of heavyweights around. There were three in particular that come to mind who would have been right there on the plane with us if they could. That's the kind of guys they were. Another thing about them was that they were three great, great champions that fought each other a bunch of times in one of the greatest of round robin wars of all time. It was the old generation- Ezzard Charles and Joe Walcott, fighting right at the end of long careers, giving way to the new generation; Rocky Marciano, who went on to become one of the greatest ever. But Ez and Joe, they didn't go down easy. They pushed their tired old bodies in there against one of the toughest guys ever to get in the ring, and they gave some of the best performances ever, against each other and against the "Rock." Now the thing is when you're up there in your thirties and you're a heavyweight you've got problems. Us little guys would do it if we could box good, but the heavies take a pounding and it takes real guts to get in there when you've slowed up.

But they did it again and again and they didn't wait a year between fights either, I mean they just didn't take time out for any soft touches like they do today. You take Frazier, Foreman, and Ali. Now there's three good champions, but I don't think there is a Charles, or a Walcott or a Marciano among them, except for Ali back when he was at his peak. It's tough to compare different generations; nobody can be very sure. Besides, it doesn't matter. They're the best today. They're champs. Now they could put on one hell of a war, but I wouldn't be surprised if there's only one or two more fights put on between them. They just can make too much money fighting nobodies where they won't get hurt.

It didn't used to be that way. You had to battle. Now, there are several kinds of battlers. There's the noisy ones like Ali. Then there's the powerful, blind-rage killer-instinct ones like Graziano. And then there's the quiet, confident but cautions ones like Ezzard Charles. Ez wasn't a real popular champion. He was kind of dull in the eyes of the fans who liked to see mayhem in the ring. The "Timid Tiger" they called him. Well, old Ez was quiet alright, but there was nothing timid about him. And he went on to show them all. Ez, he's still battling against an enemy a whole lot tougher than Rocky Marciano. And he's doing it quietly. But he's about the least timid Tiger I ever saw.

Ez was just nineteen when he turned pro in 1940. He'd had forty-two amateur fights and won them all. By the time he was seventeen he'd already won the Diamond Belt Welterweight Championship twice, plus the Golden Gloves. At eighteen he had become a middleweight and won the Diamond Belt, Golden Gloves and the A.A.U. championships. He was ready for the pros, to say the least. So he turned pro and his first year he fought fifteen times and scored twelve knockouts. He was a great boxer and in that weight class he had tremendous power, too. There's no telling what he might have done if he stopped growing. Anyway, right off the bat he had to fight the best. He was too good for anybody else, but he still didn't have much experience. He was caught in the middle. So at age twenty he lost his first fight, a close decision, to Ken Overlin, who had just lost the title to Billy Soose. But in 1942, when he was starting to reach his peak at the age of twenty-one, he knocked out former light-heavy champ, Anton Christoforidis.

Well, the war came along and Ez served a hitch in the Army, but he came back as good as ever. By now he was a light-heavyweight. There wasn't much competition in that class so he had to fight mostly heavies. But Ez was beating them all. In fact, as a light-heavy Charles beat Archie Moore three times and Joey Maxim, who later became light-heavyweight champ, five times. By this time, 1948, Ez was around Twenty-seven and he looked sure to get a heavyweight title shot.

So they were looking for opponents and this kid comes along, a light-heavyweight named Sam Baroudi who was just twenty. Now Baroudi was being played up as a fighter who had never been knocked out, so it would be a big plus for Charles for a title fight if he could knock him out. So they fought but the fight went into the tenth round. Then Ez really turned it on. I mean, he wanted that knockout. So he swarmed all over Baroudi and caught him with several lefts and rights and Baroudi went down. They carried him from the ring on a stretcher;

in the dressing room firemen tried to bring him to with an inhaler. They worked on him for forty-five minutes. Finally they took him to a hospital where he died.

Up until that time Ez had been a real tiger in the ring. But the Baroudi thing shattered him. He felt like he'd murdered the guy. He blamed himself and swore he'd never fight again. All of his friends tried to talk to him but they couldn't bring him around. Yet, a lot of the little people out there in this world are a lot bigger than people think. Ez got a telegram from Sam Baroudi's father, who was a rubber worker in Akron, Ohio. It said, "This was a terrible accident. Our family bears no bitterness at all toward you. Don't give up your career. Go on and win the championship."

And Ez did just that. But he wasn't the same fighter. He won with his great boxing ability. Some said he was holding back. They said that the ghost of Sam Baroudi was always in there with him. I don't know, it could be possible. You certainly don't know what goes on in a guy's head. But on the other hand, Ez was older now and fighting in the heavyweight division against guys who were 20-25 pounds heavier than himself half the time. If you can box good and still put a man away when there's a good opening, why stand toe to toe? Anyway, he developed the reputation and became the "Timid Tiger."

In 1949 Ez fought Gus Lesnevich, the former great light-heavyweight champion and stopped Gus in seven. He was on his way.

Now, at that time the heavyweight division was muddled. Joe Louis had retired. The national Boxing Association held an elimination series for their version of the title. This brought Ez head to head with Jersey Joe Walcott and it started 'the great heavyweight war." They fought for the first time in June, 1949, in Chicago. Now Walcott was already getting up there in age and Charles was very careful with him, figuring to wear him down and outpoint him. And it worked. He won the decision and became recognized by the National Boxing Association as the champion. That first battle of the war was a quiet one and as a result the fans didn't take to Ez. There was even some speculation about his being the true champion. Of course, his quietness didn't help any. They asked him about how it felt to be champ and he said he didn't really feel any different. Now how can a reporter put that in his column? Ez just kept his emotions to himself, which doesn't provide good copy.

But, one thing! Ez promised to be a fighting champ and that he was. Only there just wasn't anybody to fight right away. So he fought work horses like Lee Oma, Freddie Beshore, and Nick Barone, Now Joe Louis had kept active with his "bum of the month club," only Louis was a popular, exciting champion and he could get away with it. Ez's style just wasn't exciting and he became less popular.

He had his troubles. He was champ and still had a lot of fight left in him, but his career was sagging and then in 1950 the medical troubles began. The doctors discovered that there was something wrong with his heart and that he had to take it easy for a while. Therefore, they had to postpone the scheduled fight with Freddie Beshore. Then there was another exam and another postponement. Yet on his final examination the electrocardiograms indicated that he was okay. So Ez doesn't even blink. But later on he said that he was glad that he didn't lose the championship to those machines. Now that's good copy.

So in August, 1950 he fought Freddie Beshore and beat him easily. The referee stopped it later in the fourteenth for a TKO because Beshore had an ear that was swelling like a balloon. Ez was rusty and was worried over going the distance, so he didn't look too good, except when he opened up. But at least it proved his big heart was okay.

In the meantime Joe Louis was coming out of retirement because of his money problems and there was no way that there wouldn't be a Louis-Charles fight, what with the championship situation as it was. The fans would demand it. Now this was a tough thing for Ez. On the one hand, Joe was thirty-six and a good friend of his; Ez didn't want to fight him. On the other hand, Ez felt he was rusty himself and was a little worried about trading punches with Joe because of his heart. Finally business became business and the fight was set up. Now, Joe owed the government $260,000 in back taxes and he wanted to clean it up. So he offered to give his entire purse to the government for full settlement but they didn't even answer him. Consequently, Joe would have to pay taxes on his money from the Charles fight in addition, so in effect his back debt would hardly go down at all. He would simply have to keep fighting to pay for more and more taxes. As a result, Louis almost made the heavyweight picture a four man war.

The fight came off on September 27, 1950, and Charles beat him easily; but the fight went fifteen rounds to a decision which was a tribute to old Joe.

The result was that they had no choice but to universally accept Ez as champ. This the fans didn't like one bit. You see, poor Ez had just beaten one of the great American folk heroes and they wouldn't let him forget it. They said Joe was over the hill and Ez had humiliated him by letting up in the later rounds. At least he was acclaimed champion.

Ez kept busy but it didn't help his lack of popularity. In 1951 he successfully continued his war with Walcott, knocking him down in the ninth and retaining his title on a decision. That same year he knocked out Rex Layne in eleven rounds in Pittsburgh's Forbes Field. That fight told a lot. First off, the fans booed him even though he showed them the flashiest fight he'd fought in a long time. He battered the hell out of Rex in the tenth and eleventh instead of backing off. But, the funny thing was, that it cost him some of his boxing sharpness. He could handle Layne easily and might have stopped him sooner if he boxed him. Ez just seemed to have a hard time picking the right way to fight his opponent and later that same year it cost him the title when he got cautious again against Joe Walcott.

Ez floundered around for a while and he seemed to fight more cautiously than ever. He tried old Jersey Joe again in 1952, but he looked like he was going for safety first and a lot of people thought it cost him the chance to regain the title.

But the real story with Ez began in 1954. By that time the new Kid on the block, Rocky Marciano, had won the title from Jersey Joe and Rocky was the type of guy to give everybody a shot. Charles was an ex-champ so he was a logical choice and Rocky's people were sure he would be no problem. So the fight was set up for June, 1954, in Yankee Stadium.

Rocky was a seventeen to five favorite and they figured him for a knockout around the eighth round. There were around 48,000 paying customers who put down more than $700,000. They got their money's worth.

Ez came out like the Tiger he had once been and had Rocky all befuddled for the first five rounds. But Rocky was younger, much stronger, and a truly great champion. After the fifth he started getting it together. He fought out of a crouch and hammered away. By the seventh his strength took over and you could see Ez was tiring. But that's when Ez's true ring courage started to show. In the ninth Ez almost went down but he just plain refused and rocked the Rock with a wicked left hook near the end of the round. The eleventh was Rocky's best round but Ez fought him toe to toe and took the punishment and stayed on his feet. In fact, he came back and got in some good left hooks in the twelfth. But from the thirteenth on Rocky was all over him and it's a miracle he stayed on his feet. No, not a miracle, it was the Tiger in him. In the fourteenth he was shook. In the fifteenth he took a terrible beating but even so managed to sting Rocky with a couple of lefts before the final bell.

After the fight they said Ez's face looked like a grapefruit dropped from the twenty-fifth floor. Both his eyes were closed and he couldn't talk because he had taken a real tough shot to the throat. But the thing was you had two heroes that day. Rocky, who was always popular, and Ez, who had often been booed while winning.

Ezzard had been fighting for fifteen years and had hardly ever lost. But here he was a hero at last in defeat. Now, if he'd stuck and run more he might just have won. He would have been champ again, but he would have been booed. In some people's eyes he had to take a beating to be a hero. It's like Jimmy McLarnin, who was cautious and unpopular until he lost to Tony Canzoneri in 1936 when he stood toe to toe with him. Now, Jimmy had beaten thirteen former world champions but he was admired most for getting beat up. People are funny. Like I said before, if you get in the ring you're a fighter. They couldn't build steps up to the ring strong enough to hold up a coward. There are no "Timid Tigers."

Ez couldn't be with us on the plane, not that he wouldn't if he could. Ez's story doesn't end with almost beating Marciano, with tearing his nose open when they should have stopped the fight. Ez didn't complain about that and he's never complained about anything else that life's dished out for him.

But Ez started going downhill after that, and in 1959 he ended up fighting a guy who couldn't have even got on the same card with Charles five years before. This guy pummeled him and ridiculed him. It was awful. But Ez took it. The worst of it was that it was these over the hill years when Ez got TV exposure and the public saw only one tenth of the real Ezzard Charles. Three years later he was broke. Though his purses had come to almost $2 million, he had lost most of it through bad investments. He still didn't complain.

I had a couple of bad deals myself although overall I did okay. One bust was when I was fighting and my manager steered me into this Chilean oil field. That was $10,000. Then I had some nightclubs, two in Florida and one, the Melody Lane, in New York City. The trouble wasn't with the clubs but with my partners. For instance, the Melody Lane was great and I was making money for about a year, but my partner, who was a "great chef", didn't want to cook. Naturally, the kitchen went to pot. Too bad he couldn't serve it. His thing was to hang around the lounge where he could watch the girls and catch the action; as it got later the food would get worse. I left.

About my only other bad investment was in a tavern I bought in Hartford. In fact, I only got involved in it to keep Pop busy. It was a pretty good location and for the first three weeks I worked the place to get it going. While I was there we made money but after that I had to leave my father alone with the place, and the trouble started. Each week after I left he started asking me for six or seven hundred dollars because the place was now in the red. He was no businessman and if you came in and said, "Willie Pep was a great guy and a Great Fighter," you ate and drank for nothing; and if you didn't say nice things he would ask you to leave. Pop also figured everybody in the world should eat Italian food; but everyone around there was Irish, and so they started staying away. When the place would get empty Pop would get sleepy, being all alone; so he'd lock up and go to sleep in the back room. Half the time you couldn't get in if you wanted to. We gave it up along with about $15,000.

You can't complain about these things and Charles didn't complain either, even though it hurt. In the early sixties Ezzard was stricken and hospitalized. They found out that he had amyotrophic lateral sclerosis. And more likely it had been already affecting him during those downhill years. It's the same disease that took Lou Gehrig, only it got Ez in the legs first instead of the upper body. When he could still talk he used to say that he was lucky because he didn't have any pain.

Yet things got worse for him. They took away his house. And he had to sell his cars for food.

But Ez pulled himself together at first and went to work for the Chicago Youth Commission, talking to underprivileged kids and consulting with officials. They paid him a salary and he and his family got by. But Ez's legs got worse and worse and he had to use a walking gadget to get around. But they didn't forget Ez. In 1968 they had an affair for him in Chicago and almost 1300 people were there, including Rocky Marciano, Archie Moore and Muhammad Ali. They gave him a check for $15,000. Everybody made speeches. Ez could only whisper, Thank you, thank you, thank you."

Rocky Marciano summed up the whole thing. "I never fought a man like Ez before in my life. Ez, you fought me about the best of anybody. I couldn't put you down and I don't think anybody can put you down. You've got more spirit than any man I ever knew." After Rocky's death in 1969 they found in his memoirs that he called Ezzard Charles the most underrated fighter of all time.

Ez has been in a wheelchair for the past six years. He's about fifty-two now. His wife Gladys does his talking for him and has to hand feed him and lift him, with the help of his nineteen-year-old son Ezzard II, to a tilt table for exercise. But Ez still isn't complaining. His smile is as quick as ever. Like I said, he's the least "Timid Tiger" I ever met.

ROUND 13

"JERSEY JOE"

OF THE THREE GUYS THAT FOUGHT each other so tough, Jersey Joe Walcott is the only one who had any luck after he left the ring. Yet, in the ring Joe was sort of unlucky with his timing. He was a great fighter who got stuck in Joe Louis' shadow for a good part of his career. But Jersey Joe was tough, and like Jimmy Braddock, he came off the relief rolls and became the heavyweight champion of the world.

Besides his own title defenses, he was a contender at least six times that I can think of. Joe was great and even though he got his chances late he got plenty of them. He just couldn't be denied.

His first shot came against Joe Louis in 1947 and he almost won it then. He dropped the "Brown Bomber" in the fourth round, but Louis got up and beat him in a close decision. In fact, a lot of people thought Jersey Joe had whipped him. But to beat the champion you've got to beat him decisively. Titles don't change hands on a few points. And that's the way it should be.

Ruby Goldstein was the referee in that fight and he had disagreed with the judges and given Joe Walcott the decision. So a couple of weeks later when Ruby was refereeing a Friday night fight, Joe was at ringside to be introduced. Now, normally when you're introduced you shake hands with the fighter first and then the referee. But Joe rushed over to Ruby and grabbed his hand with both hands and with a big smile on his face nearly breaks it off pumping it.

That fight was really the first big TV fight because quite a few people were getting sets about that time, although most didn't until around 1949. But there were plenty of TV stores and crowds gathered on sidewalks all over the country to watch it through the store windows or in the bars.

I happened to be in New York City at the time, and my friend, Larry asked me over to his West Side apartment to play a little cards and watch the fight on his new "Tele-tone" set.

I got there about seven-thirty that night and played cards until almost fight time, with Larry and his three pals. I was ahead a couple of hundred bucks. Larry decided that we should have a snack while watching the fight so we called the neighborhood deli for some sandwiches.

It was round three in the bout when the doorbell rang. One of the guys got up and walked from the parlor through the dining room to the front door. He let the delivery boy in and then both came back into the parlor. The delivery "boy," a sleazy looking character of about fifty, placed the bag of food on the table and gave me the bill since I was the closest one to him.

It came to about six or seven dollars; so I picked a ten dollar bill from my pot on the table, gave it to him and told him to keep the change.

The guy, knowing who I was, said, "Thanks Willie. I watch a lot of your fights, I think you're great." Like the other guys, I was interested in Louis and Walcott blasting away on the TV screen and so I said thanks without looking up.

For some reason I turned a few seconds later and the guy was still there and he was dipping his hand into my pot. I said, "Hey, what are you doing? Leave that money alone." The guy got as red as a beet and made a dash for the door, still holding onto some of the money. He ran through the dining room and when he reached a door, he turned the doorknob and rammed through. By this time Larry and his pals got there with me and we all started to laugh. The "delivery boy" had mistaken the closet for the front door. He was a different kind of a crook.

127

The guy from inside the closet says, "Please, I didn't mean it," and slips the money he took under the door. He had picked up about forty-five dollars. I said, "alright, come out and we won't hurt you." Silence. Then I tried to open the door but the guy was pulling from the other side and it wouldn't budge. I told him that we wanted to watch the fight and for him to get out peacefully. More silence. Then we noticed some water coming out from under the door. It turned out that the guy was so scared he wet his pants. I guess he had cause with a fighter and the other guys no slouches.

However, we couldn't call the police even if we wanted to because it was illegal to have a friendly card game; so we didn't try to scare him with that. Larry seeing that this guy might do more damage to his closet, threatened to break the door and really beat him.

The guy finally let go and the door opened. He was wet from the waist down and he had his hands over his face, repeating his "Please, don't hit me" lines. We got back to the fight for the twelfth round.

But what do you think? This guy went back and told his boss at the deli that Willie Pep roughed him up for kicks. Here the guy tried to steal my money, he dirtied Larry's apartment and then he says that he was roughed up by me. I guess the guy had to save his job. But there was no bad press or talk about it anymore or any rumors that Willie Pep roughs up fifty-year-old "delivery boys." When you're in the public eye things are played up pretty big, true or false.

It's like the reputation I got for being an avid dice player. I've played lots of dice but not the way people thought. As a kid twelve or thirteen in Hartford I used to play "chickee" for crap games. That means the guy running the game would plant me in a spot where I could spot the police if they came; and if so I'd run like the wind and warn them. They would pay me a couple of bucks which was big money in the thirties.

The dice reputation grew from an incident that happened back when I was champ. I was in Hartford and had gone to look for a friend of mine who was in the woods of a parade ground playing dice. I didn't want to play; I just wanted to see him because I happened to be in town. In the woods there's six guys including my friend and I happened to be there. Naturally, I didn't run and they picked me up. The next day the papers played it big- "Willie Pep caught in crap game". Like I said,

I played dice once in a while but never to the extent of playing "in the woods".

I was never able to live it down and people got the impression that I went looking for crap games. It got so bad that for example many times while walking in New York guys would approach me and tell me about some great crap game in progress. While staying in hotels I would get calls from strangers about some hot crap game in some room.

Anyway, I've digressed far too long. Walcott got a second chance about six months later, but Louis knocked him out in the eleventh round. That turned out to be Joe Louis' last great fight. He subsequently fought some exhibitions and then retired in March, 1949.

That, of course, left the title open and, like I said, Jersey got beat by Charles for the title in June of that year. But Jersey Joe was tough and still can hit with tremendous power. In 1950, when he knocked out Harold Johnson, they had to take him out on a stretcher.

So Joe was back in 1951, and Charles out cautioned him to retain the title. But that didn't stop Joe. In July of that year they fought for the third time in Pittsburgh's Forbes Field. Now, at that time, Joe was already thirty-seven years old and most fighters, especially heavyweights, have hung them up by then. But Joe was still sharp and very powerful; beside, he knew his business, and that old son-of-a-gun set up Ezzard for a sucker punch in the seventh round and knocked him out. The man was thirty-seven, the oldest to ever gain the championship.

There was supposed to be a return fight in sixty days, but they said that Charles' people didn't want it that quick. Ez had been too careful the last time and let Walcott hang in there long enough to get in that good shot. But Joe's people didn't want it either. They figured the guy was old and that if he lost that would be the end. They figured they'd cash in on public appearances using his name and title, hoping to come up with at least three or four hundred thousand dollars. They showed Joe that in seven years Jack Dempsey had made two and a half million through refereeing and public appearances, and so Joe went along with it. However, Joe didn't have that super public image either, so it didn't work out. It takes a showman, I guess, like an Ali, to get away with that. During that time, Charles was fighting and Joe was getting older. However, when they finally fought in 1952 Charles got too cautious with Joe again, remembering that punch from the last fight. Consequently, Joe was good enough and smart enough to win that decision.

That set it up for Rocky Marciano to enter the picture. On September 23, 1952, as the first Charles-Marciano fight was a great one, so was the first Walcott-Marciano fight. The kid from Massachusetts seemed to bring out the best in the old timers; it was as if they gathered some secret strength in an attempt to show that their generation of fighters were the best. Well, they fought and it was some brawl. Age against youth, boxer against slugger. In the first minute Joe floored Rocky with a wicked express train left hook. Now that was the first time Rocky had ever been down and the fans were shocked. Rocky got up at four more mad than hurt and charged Joe. Everybody figured Joe would stick and run but he didn't; he stood in there and they went at it toe to toe. In the second round, Rocky's knees sagged and he almost went down. But in the third, fourth, and fifth Rocky charged as usual and started getting old Joe on the ropes where he could bang away at his midsection. However, Joe would slip away and do some scoring of his own.

Then in the 6th they banged heads; Joe got a cut eyebrow and Rocky tore his forehead open. That created lots of trouble. Rocky's cut man applied medication and somehow, probably from the sweating, it got in his eye. Rocky ended up fighting a shadow. So slick old Joe concentrated on staying away, working the cut. For the next three rounds Rocky took an awful beating and in the following rounds Joe piled up points. By the time they reached the end of twelve Joe had to be knocked out to lose.

But before the fight Joe had said, "If I don't whip him, take my name off the record book." So, old Jersey went into the thirteenth over-confident. Rocky had one eye closed and was cut over the other one, but he just refused to lose on points. He knew the only way to get an opening was to give one himself and take a chance on being knocked out. He moved Joe into the ropes, dropped his left hand low, and feinted with his shoulder. Sure enough, Joe started a left and then Rocky threw the perfect punch; an overhand right that didn't travel much more than a foot. It seemed as it if exploded on Joe's jaw. He was out before he hit the canvas. Joe just laid there with his arms across the ropes and forehead on the floor. He didn't even twitch. He was out cold for a full thirty seconds. If they had a book to teach boxing that punch would have been right from the book.

That was one of the greatest fights ever and yet Jersey Joe Walcott was thirty-eight at the time. He had been ahead on all cards against the "Brockton Blockbuster," until that one murderous punch. Just one punch. Without it ring history might have been completely different.

Joe fought on for a while, fighting Rocky again in fact. But age had taken its toll and he had to retire. But like so many fighters, he didn't quit fighting. Joe got up on a soap box and got himself elected sheriff of Camden, New Jersey. Joe, who headed many kid programs in the New Jersey area, still helps with benefits whenever he can. He still keeps in close touch with Ezzard. Joe couldn't make this one particular benefit because of his duties, but I know he was with us in spirit.

ROUND 14

"THE BROCKTON BLOCKBUSTER"

SO WITH THE OLD HEROES WHIPPED, Rocky Marciano took charge or at least his manager did. Rocky, who was born Rocco Marchegiano, needed promoting like the rest of us. And his manager, Al Weill, was one shrewd guy. At one point in his career, Rocky had been coming along well, but he hadn't really fought anybody important. His manager then decided he needed to whip a big name to earn a title shot. In 1951 Weill and promoter Jim Norris brought Joe Louis out of retirement again as a set-up for the Rock.

But old Joe was tougher than they expected and hung in there until the eighth round when Rocky finally knocked him out.

Now, the thing was that Joe was washed up by then and had no business being in there, and Rocky knew it, too. He felt real bad about it, but Rocky didn't hold back. The old man did pretty good but it was just a matter of time until Rocky would knock him out. Rocky felt sick about it for Joe had been his boyhood boxing idol. Rocky actually got sick to his stomach. That's the kind of guy he was.

Anyway, Rocky's problem was that there just wasn't anyone around to fight. All of the name fighters were old and he had already beaten most of them. But the old guys didn't give up easily. Old Jersey

 132

Joe tried again but he was just too old and got knocked out with one punch in the first round of the return bout.

And so did Ezzard Charles. Now that fight was really promoted. In 1954 the International Boxing Commission wanted the fight in one of the ball parks in New York for September. You see, all of the New York teams were in contention and a fight there would have drawn all the out-of-towners who were in for the World Series. There was a lot of excitement also over the first fight and the promoters thought they'd end up with a million dollar gate, the first since the Louis-Conn fight in 1946. However, Al Weill didn't want Rocky to fight again in 1954 for tax reasons.

They did eventually fight again, and it was a good fight, too; Charles wasn't finished yet. In the seventh Round he split Rocky's nose open to the bone. By this time Rocky's nose was a famous target. In fact, in a sparring session when he was training for the Walcott return, Rocky got his nose puffed up. The doctors said it was a deviated septum, and the bout was postponed. Anyway, here he was in with Charles and his nose was bleeding so bad that if he didn't put Charles away in a hurry they'd have to stop it. So Rocky went out there in the eighth and he was all over Ezzard. Rocky knew he had to knock him out quick and he came through in championship form.

The only other guy around was Archie Moore, the great light-heavyweight champion, only he was over the hill, too. But they fought anyway in 1955, and believe it or not, old Archie knocked Rocky down. But he was floored four times himself and finally knocked out in the ninth round.

That was just about it. He fought everybody else who wanted a shot but there wasn't any competition. His fight with Don Cockell, the British Empire Champion, was better than most. Cockell was a real roly-poly guy but he was courageous. He took some tremendous shots but was actually outscoring Rocky through the first six rounds. That was typical. The Rock was no boxer and wasn't really a one punch knockout guy either, but he'd keep coming and you just couldn't hurt him. If you did, it would just make him mad and he was one guy who could fight better when he got mad. He'd catch one or two to hit you three or four times and he'd hurt you a lot worse than you could hurt him. Anyway, Cockell shook Rocky in the sixth, but that was it. From then on it was Rocky's and he finally knocked him out in the ninth round.

Rocky was undefeated against the great old timers and everybody else. But there was no one left to fight so he retired at age thirty-two. He had won forty-nine bouts, no losses and forty-three knockouts. He had revitalized the division just like Joe Louis had done fifteen years earlier. If Rocky doesn't go down as one of the greatest ever it will be because there just wasn't enough competition for him. Maybe if the Rock had come back and won some more fights he would have been considered the best. I don't know, but I do know he must have felt that he could beat Patterson and the guys he beat. He wouldn't say it though. Rocky never knocked a fighter in his life, and he never made a prediction. That just wasn't part of him.

Anyway, there had been a lot of talk about a comeback, but Rocky had retired in good shape financially and was enjoying retirement. Sure he had thought about fighting again, but he knew that only he and Gene Tunney had quit with any fight left at all. He was on top and wanted it to stay that way.

Now they say in 1957 Jim Norris offered him a million dollars to come back, spread out over a few years for tax purposes. That's a terrific temptation, and of course, the Rock had to be thinking about being the first man ever to regain the heavyweight championship. However, he also knew that if he lost he would be downgraded and they didn't come any prouder than Rocky.

They also said that Rocky was offered in 1959 $3 million to come back against Patterson. He'd seen guys like Roy Harris and Pete Rademacher drop Patterson and must have figured he could whip him. But Rocky was thirty-six by then and he couldn't forget about Dempsey, Schmelling, Louis, Charles and Walcott who had all tried and failed. Another thing, he was enjoying retirement and training would have taken him away from his family for at least six months. Finally, Rocky didn't need the money; so Rocky stayed retired.

The guys in the plane weren't talking much; being Christmas Eve they had their minds on their families. I did, to, but being in the jet made me recall my accident in 1947.

January 5th it was. I was champion of the world and I was in Miami, Florida, when my manager, Lou Viscusi, called me. He said, "Gee, Willie, you better get back to Hartford and start training. You've got to fight in three and a half weeks." It was the height of the season and I couldn't get a reservation on the scheduled flights. So I got a seat on a non-scheduled airline- a two motor job.

We left at four in the afternoon with twenty-one of us on the plane heading for Newark. The weather was okay when we left Florida, but as soon as we moved into the Northeast it began to snow.

When we reached Newark we began to circle. We circled so long that I started to doze and finally fell asleep. Then all of a sudden I woke up to the cries, screams and moans of the passengers. The plane had crashed. The pilot had tried to land but the visibility was so poor that he overshot the field and landed in a wooded area in Middleville, New Jersey.

The plane rammed through the trees like a charging fullback, ripping the plane apart.

I was lying face down and couldn't move; my back and legs were paralyzed. I couldn't help anyone and they couldn't help me; we were all hurt and in shock.

My entire life flashed in my mind like a newsreel in a matter of seconds. I didn't know how serious my condition was, but thought of being through in the fight game terrified me. I was alive-but would I be able to box again?

I don't know how long it was as we waited to be rescued, but it felt like a lifetime. When they did arrive they put me on a stretcher and set us all in a makeshift ambulance.

There were five people killed, including the pilot and nearly everyone was seriously hurt.

They drove us to a hospital at a small Army base in nearby Middleville. It was an old hospital on an old base, but is was adequate for the emergency. On the way there, I overheard a guy who was helping in the ambulance say, "That's Willie Pep, but he isn't going to fight anymore." Those words cut like knives. I couldn't bear to hear it. However, thanks to good fortune and others five months later I was boxing once again.

Anyway, Rocky started his boxing career late, and had his first professional fight when he was twenty-four years old, about five years later than the average professional boxer. Rocky had been pursuing a baseball career as a catcher but had to give it up after an arm injury. His next best sport was boxing.

Chuck Davey lands right to Chico Vejar's eye - 1952   N.Y. Daily News

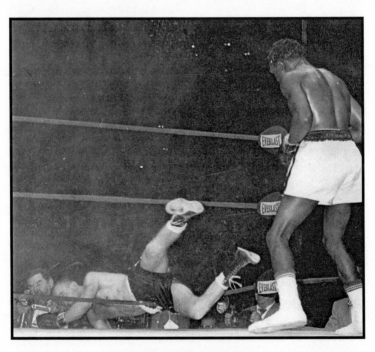

Chuck Davey the T.V. hero falls. Gavilan retains title - 1953
N.Y. Daily News

 136

Middleweights Ernie Durando and Paddy Young - N.Y. Daily News

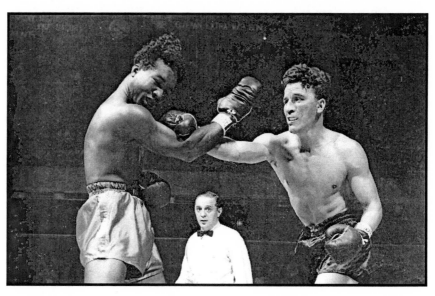

Tippy Larkin (R) beats Willie Joyce for Jr. Welterweight title - 1946

N.Y. Daily News

Middleweights Rocky Castellani (L) and Ernie Durando - 1951

N.Y. Daily News

Rocky Graziano charges Charley Fusari in last minute of 10th round to stop Fusari (L) – 1949   N.Y. Daily News

Willie getting ready for Champ Hogan Bassey - 1958   N.Y. Daily News

Freddie Russo lands a left hook to the belly on his way to a victory over Nick Stato - 1948 Providence Journal News Photo

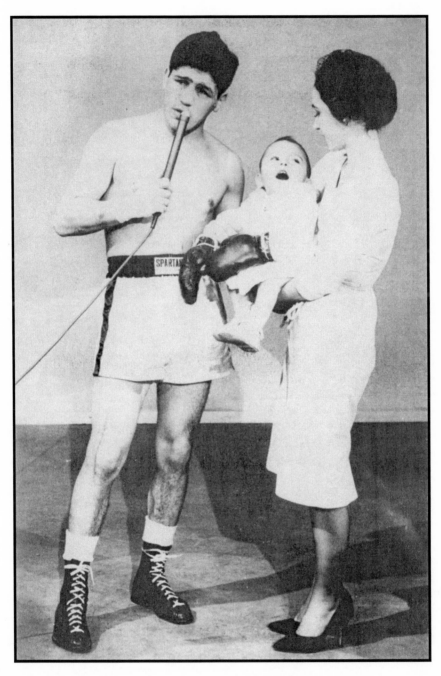

Chico Vejar with little Jimmy and wife Caryl - 1961

pic. 48 Former boxing greats at a benefit for retarded children at Philadelphia's Spectrum Arena – 1972. (L-R Sitting) Frank Franconeri, Freddie Russo, Carmen Basilio, Tippy Larkin and Chuck Davey, (Middle row) Willie Pep, Carmen Giardello, Joey Giardello, Charlie Fusari, Billy Graham, Rocky Graziano and Chico Vejar. (rear) Al Certo, Jake LaMotta, Bat Battalino, Paul Pender, Ernie Durando, Sandy Saddler, Billy Conn, Larry Forte, Dan Bucceroni and Eddie Giosa

*shot of fighters in costumes
– Chico Vejar, Willie and Joey
Archer at Appalachia –*

*another shot of fighters in
costumes*

3rd shot in costumes

MEET THE VOICE

Announcer Johnnie Addie raises hand of Light heavyweight Champ
Joey Maxim

 146

Joe Walcott (R) connects and drops Joe Louis with left hooks to the jaw - 1947
N.Y. Daily News

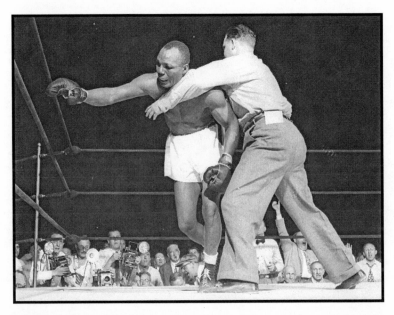

Joe Walcott kayoed by Joe Louis in return bout - 1948 N.Y. *Daily News*

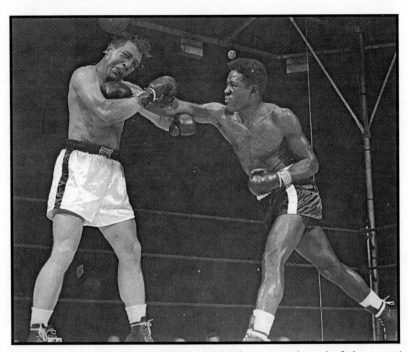

Ezzard Charles kayoes Gus Lesnevich in heavyweight title fight - 1949
- N.Y. Daily News

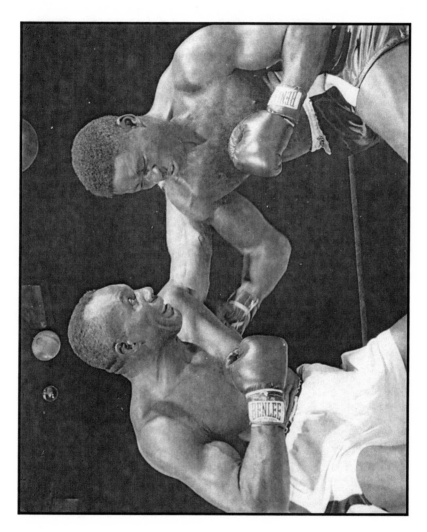

Ezzard Charles beats Joe Walcott for Title - 1949   N.Y. Daily News

Rocky Maricano kayoes former Champion Joe Louis – 1951 N.Y. Daily News

Walcott beats Marciano to the punch - 1952   N.Y. Daily News

Marciano beats Charles in title fight - 1954   N.Y. Daily News

Marciano's nose cut to the bone, moves in on Charles - 1954   N.Y. Daily News

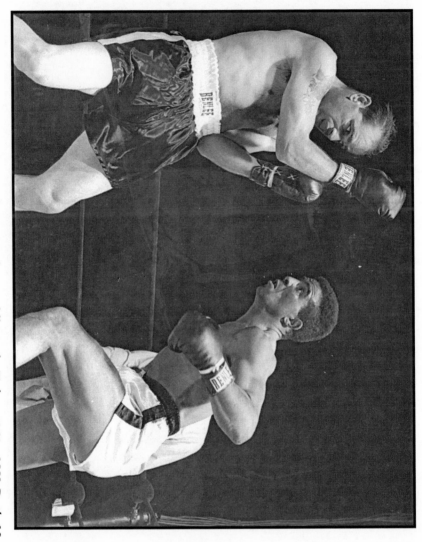

Bobo Olson (L) beats England's Randy Turpin for middleweight Title – 1953   N.Y. Daily News

Johnny Arcaro, Joey Adams, Cindy Adams & Jack Dempsey at Jack Dempsey's Restaurant

Pep and Babe Ruth -
"The Sultan of Swat" Babe Ruth with Willie in Miami, Fl 1946

It took 26 spectacular years to build the legend of Willie Pep. And now that the building stage has been completed everybody agrees...

They'll never Forget LITTLE WILLIE

Johnny Brannigan

His first sixteen bouts were all won by kayoes and by 1950 he descended on New York's Madison Square Garden like a storm. He knocked out Carmine Vingo and then won a decision from highly touted Roland La Starza. Rocky was on his way.

In his bout with Vingo, he hit him so hard that Carmine was seriously hurt, ending his boxing career. Rocky mentioned this bout to me several times, saying he felt very bad about Carmine.

Rocky, as a fighter, had tremendous discipline in training and gave orders that he would accept calls only from his wife- providing it was an emergency. His almost superhuman strength and his desire to win made his 5'11" "granite" frame as indestructible as a "Sherman Tank." Rocky was totally involved in his profession and his attitude is a model for any kid to follow, even today.

I was as close to Rocky as anyone. We spent a lot of time together in Florida where Rocky vacationed with his family. We had a good lot in common, and we were also born under the same Zodiac sign-Virgo- as was another Italian, Christopher Columbus.

I didn't get to know Rocky until around 1950. When we got to be friends he told me a story about how he followed me one time. He was just starting out in 1947 and I was champion of the world. He spotted me sitting in Jack Dempsey's with a young lady. He said that he wanted to come over and introduce himself but he felt shy. After a while I left with the girl and headed down to Times Square to catch a movie. I didn't know it, but Rocky and his trainer Allie Columbo were tailing me to see "what a champion of the world does and where he goes." Well, I disappointed Rocky. He followed me to the string of second run theatres on 42nd street and then saw me vanish into one of the theaters with the girl. Rocky figured I would take her to some exclusive nightclub.

He told me this story a few years later and was even able to tell me what movie was playing, Whisperin' Smith with Alan Ladd, he said in his New England accent.

Rocky, a great and popular champion with people of all ages, made countless personal appearances throughout the country and abroad. Many times, when he was unable to make it, he would say to them, "Willie Pep, he'll make it for me," and then call and give me the details.

It was the wee hours of the morning on August 31, 1969, when Johnny Arcaro phoned me from New York City. He told me that Rocky had been killed in a charter flight that crashed over Newton, Iowa, while enroute to a personal appearance. I didn't answer Johnny or even bother to put the phone back on the receiver, I cried like a baby. I had lost "my friend."

There have been so many good things that have been said about Rocky- of his greatness in the ring and his gentleness as a human being. But for me, the guy who really summed it up several years ago was Rocky's great trainer, the late Charlie Goldman. Charlie had a contract with Rocky's manager Al Weill that called for him to get 10 percent of the net purses of Rocky's bouts. For the first couple of years Charlie got his 10 per cent, but when Rocky got into the big money bouts Weill started to pay Charlie much less. One day Charlie explained this to Rocky and Rocky agreed that this was not right. He took it upon himself to talk it over with Weill. When Rocky walked into Weill's office and told him that Charlie should get his 10 per cent because it was the original agreement, Weill just looked at Rocky, like a cat. Then he stood up and walked towards him and said, "Rocky, your business is fighting so don't get involved in my affairs with Goldman,"

He then slapped Rocky across the face.

For a few seconds Rocky looked at Weill, a rotund 5'4" middle aged man, and then simply and quietly walked out.

ROUND 15

"APPALACHIA"

It seemed like no time at all until I felt the plane dip a wing. You know how it feels. You kind of get pinned to your seat and feel rather helpless. I mean, if something was wrong there was nothing I could do about it anyway. I just looked out the window. I could see that we were pretty low right over the mountains. It felt good to know that the pilot was Perry Hoisington, a retired two-star General. I felt that he knew what he was doing, even if I didn't. As we banked I saw those dead mountains, no sign of life. Those mountains used to be beautiful until they scraped half the tops off them looking for coal. Now they looked cold and still. It made me uncomfortable to think that there were real people stuck down there with absolutely nothing. But that's what our trip was about.

Chico had got the whole thing started a couple of weeks before, he had read a lot about Appalachia and it had "got" to him. A lot of people will say things like, "Gee, those poor people in Appalachia, somebody ought to do something about it." They sort of enjoy feeling sorry for them. But no more. But not Chico. He said, "I ought to do something about it." And he did it. Guys like Chico and Joey Giardello are special.

 159

There's always a lot of work involved, even when you want to help someone. I mean, he couldn't just get on an airplane and go down there.

Chico started the whole thing at Leone's Restaurant in New York. He had a lot of business and press people in the audience and he ran down the trip for them. You probably have never heard Chico talk, but let me say that he's dynamite. I mean the guy puts his heart and soul into it and people respond and with their donations as well. He told them how he had contacted the different health agencies down there and had asked them to help him find the people with the really serious problems, the handicapped poor, for example. Chico had seen first-hand what being handicapped is all about and how much caring for people means. And he figured that being pressed down by poverty and ignorance and being handicapped on top of it, you just had to find somebody that cared. It was close to Christmas and he had made up his mind that those people would find that somebody did care.

When he contacted the different agencies he got replies from the Cerebral Palsy, Heart Disease, Polio and Leukemia people. We would be visiting a hospital and going to some private homes, too. Chico got a list of what was needed: wheelchairs and braces, etc. He also learned what clothes sizes were needed for the individual family members and also the ages of the kids for toys. We even sent twin beds to one family. They had a handicapped daughter and what little money was left over from their food bills had to go to her; so their two sons had to sleep on mattresses on the floor. And it's cold down there.

Chico got everything together and most of the stuff was shipped on down ahead of us. What money was left over was sent to the local agencies to buy food.

When we landed at this airport on top of a mountain in Pottsville, Pennsylvania, there were hundreds of people lined up waiting to welcome us. It was amazing, my feeling funny about the elf suit lasted about two seconds. I waved and the people cheered. You couldn't help but feel good.

There some officials from the Heart Association picked us up and took us to Ashland State Hospital; that was Chico, Joey Archer, Steve Belloise and me. Joey Giardello took the other guys to a different town so we'd cover more ground. Ashland State Hospital. Now I'd seen some state hospitals before, usually big old brick things that look something like prisons.

Really cold. Well, this place was old, all right, maybe seventy to eighty years old. But instead of being a "big old Brick thing" it was just a big old wooden house. It was bare and needed repairs but the nuns who ran it did their dandiest to keep the place clean and cheery. It was the State Hospital for little kids with heart disease; kids between the ages of four and twelve. These kids were really poor and poverty makes you weak anyway, so when your heart isn't in top shape you're in even bigger trouble.

The nuns told us that we could go ahead and pop into the wards as Santa and his helpers, but that we should be careful not to overdo it. We weren't to get the kids too excited. It wasn't easy, you know. Santa Claus gets anybody excited, including little elves.

How those kids eyes lit up. Chico was Santa Claus with his great big sack of toys and stuff, and we were his little "helpers." Ginks and me as elves, and Joey Archer as a clown. The kids loved us. They each got pajamas, slippers, a robe and, of course toys. Chico made sure that the toys weren't the real exciting kind; more of the kind to keep them busy, but quiet. We had paint sets and coloring books, it didn't seem like much, but most of them had never even had that much before. I'm telling you, to them it was the happiest Christmas ever. And when I looked at the other guys I could see they were having the same problem I was, keeping back the tears.

Before we left the hospital the people treated us to a buffet. Now we were hungry all right, but it just didn't seem right. But that's the way just about everybody we met was. Why, even the poorest families, if they had two pieces of bread, they'd give you one of them.

The Cerebral Palsy volunteers picked us up at the hospital and drove us 20 miles to a place called Minersville where we visited a family with a six-year old boy who suffered from Cerebral Palsy. His name was Jerry. His father was out of work like just about everybody else down there. They managed because he would go to the abandoned mines to dig up coal and drive 25 miles to sell it on his own.

When we arrived and they called Jerry from the bedroom, when he saw us his eyes lit up. You just could see some life take hold of him and he walked 10 feet to greet us, the farthest he had walked up to that time. We had toys for him, stuff he had only dreamed about, and some special equipment. We had coats for his twelve-and fourteen-year-old sisters, who were wearing no more than rags for warmth. Most kids might get new coats because styles change, but these kids *really* needed them. Chico had them bought at Lord & Taylor's and the kids just couldn't wait to get back to school to show them off. They had never seen coats like that, except in catalogues.

We made some more stops and it was the same thing over and over. Dirt poor, but proud people who accepted us graciously. And smiling kids with weak little bodies.

We met with Joey's group back at the airport and flew on to East Philadelphia. People from the Leukemia Association picked us up and we went to the home of a little girl who was retarded and had leukemia.

We had bright dresses for her and toys that made lots of noise. Simple things that she could understand. She was so overcome that she came out of her shell and played with us. Retarded children need more stimulation than other children, but poverty doesn't allow for it. The parents were very grateful.

The flight to Newark took twelve and a half minutes; nobody said a word. We were all deep in our own thoughts. Yes, the next day the sun would come up and there would still be poverty and suffering. Yet we all hoped that we brought them a little sunshine. One hears about poverty but it doesn't hit home until you see it. Pottsville. Minersville. Appalachia is a different world. The mines and mills are closed; the towns are crumbling and they even have large abandoned sections that are simply off limits. It's even worse out of town: no electricity, no running water, no heat, except for a wood stove. The clothes are third generation hand-me-downs. The cars are from the thirties, and most of them just sit there rusting in front yards. There's no money for gas.

It was only a few hours before Christmas when we got off the plane. Joey Giardello left with the Jersey guys, Fusari, Larkin and Durando. Tiger Jones drove back to Queens. Chico Vejar dropped off Ginks and Joey Archer in the Bronx on his way back to Stamford. And I had that long drive back to Wethersfield.

I still had my costume on and I felt kind of like little elf in the dark. I turned up my coat collar against the cold and headed into the night. In the parking lot my car was off to the side. As I was about to get in I yelled.

"Merry Christmas, ya lousy bums."

"THE LAST TIME AROUND"

THE THREE-HOUR DRIVE SEEMED LIKE A long drive now after the flurry of the benefits, the kids, and the flight home. Day-dreaming always fills in the time.

When I was fifteen an older kid had taken me aside and told me to pretend that a cop was chasing me in the ring. Don't get caught, he said. Hit and run. That became my philosophy throughout my career. Not getting hit as a fighter helps, amateur or professional. I was champion of the world for nine years, longer than any other featherweight. I was able to fight when I was forty-four years old, and I could run six furlongs in about 1:09.

The human body can take just so much. Now punchers don't last as long as boxers. I remember seeing a fight between Sugar Ray and Carmen Basilio, who was a tough fighter and strong as a bull. Yet, Robinson hit him more in one round than I got hit in fifty of my fights. Basilio didn't last that long, but Robinson fought until he was forty-five because he was a great boxer and didn't get hit that often.

As a kid I grew up in a neighborhood where it was tough to be small. When I was shining shoes and the neighborhood kids would pick on me I'd get cornered in an alley and I'd have to fight, and those bigger kids would whip me. So I went to the local gym and asked to be taught. I was so skinny that they kicked me out. But I came back a couple of days later with my headgear and they let me stay. Well, I got knocked down nine times a day, but I learned. I was determined.

But that was a long time ago. I'm fifty-one now! and still 5'6". Times have changed. Friday night in New York, the place would be alive with sports people and writers. Toots Shor's was a big hangout, being right near the old Roxy theater on 52nd Street. Sports writers would come before and after the fights. There would be plenty of sports figures around, too. Guys like Duke Snider, Joe DiMaggio, and Johnny Mize. And guys, when they were in town, like Ted Williams and "Hammering" Hank Greenberg. Football players and basketball players, boxers and wrestlers, guys that were real genuine heroes to their fans. But that was long ago. It just doesn't seem the same anymore. Maybe I'm just getting old.

As I said, after the Saddler fights I continued to win but I did not get to be champ again. I was an ex-champ and ex-champs fight in the sticks. I became a Duncan Hines on Diners, eating in all kinds of one arm joints in places like Peoria and hanging around bus depots at night waiting for a bus connection to Kansas by way of some place I never heard of. Even when you're making a comeback you've got to fight ordinary opponents and that means small towns. You have to get there three or four days before the fight so they can play it up in the local press. When it's over you pack up and go home and wait for another match. And so I was fighting in Aiken, South Carolina, Lawton, Oklahoma, and Presque Isle, Maine.

It got lonely being an ex-champ, but I was determined. I kept fighting and fighting and I would have kept fighting until I was eighty, if possible. Finally I got my chance in 1958 when I had my fight with Hogan "Kid" Bassey, the then featherweight champ. If I were to win I was to get a shot at the title again. Now I was thirty-seven at the time and it wasn't easy to get in shape anymore. Yet I got in shape. I was in there boxing really good and not feeling my age. "I'm winning, I'm winning," I said to myself. "Just keep it up." For eight rounds it was pretty easy. Then in the ninth he caught me on the chin with an overhand left and I went down. Bassey, a Nigerian, had a tremendous one-punch wallop, and after another knockdown, the referee stopped it.

That ended the chance for the championship. I had one more fight the following year in Caracas, Venezuela, with a guy called Sonny Leon. He didn't touch me for five or six rounds. In the seventh he knocked me down and naturally he got that round. The eighth and ninth were perhaps even, but I won the tenth hands down. Leon won by a decision.

Any American boy that goes overseas wasn't going to get a decision. I thought I had won that fight, but who was I to argue with these people. I got on a plane the next day and left. I announced my retirement after this bout. It was 1959.

In November, 1964, I was in Florida with a horse owner and another kid named Artie who was an ex-fighter. Artie had been pretty good but he had quit because he wasn't getting along with his wife. At that time Artie came to me and said, "Willie, I want to fight again and I want you to handle me." I said no at first, but he talked me into it. His manager, Mike Marino, and I started him working out in the local gym and doing roadwork.

Artie was booked to fight in a six rounder for January 20, 1965, in Miami, but two weeks before the fight Artie became very ill. Mike was on a spot with the promoter and he tried to think of almost anything. Then he looked at me and said, "Willie do me a favor." I agreed. When Mike went to the promoter to tell them about the switch, they didn't holler one bit. They loved it. They figured on a bigger gate.

So I boxed with the understanding that it was an exhibition and got $1500. It was my first fight in six years. It felt pretty good.

The promoter talked to me about some other exhibitions and four weeks later I boxed again. This time not an exhibition but an eight round bout with a tough kid named Hal McKeever in Miami, I won and was on my way again.

I remember the day after the exhibition. I was back in the gym going hot and heavy against a husky young welterweight. After the workout I laid on the dressing room table and asked a guy there how far Key West was from Miami where the promoters had me already booked for another fight. The guy said, "Willie, that ain't so far." Then I said, "Tell me how far is it from Miami to Madison Square Garden?" The guy then shook his head and said, "Too far, Willie, Much too far for you."

I boxed in Providence, Ottawa, Arizona and Philadelphia. I got a guy named George Shepard as an agent, and Mike was in my corner; it wasn't too bad.

Shepard would hustle fights for me. Now he knew I was forty-five so he didn't put me in against real top fighters. He'd put me in against guys who were over the hill like myself or kids that were just starting out. I would out-fumble the old guys and outsmart the kids. So I made a few bucks and didn't get hurt. But in one of my fights in 1965 I boxed a tough kid named Tommy Haden in Providence who was the junior lightweight champion of New England. There I thought I had bit off a little more than I could chew. Rocky Graziano was the referee. The first couple of rounds looked like it was going to be a real tough fight. Maybe I could have gone ten rounds with him, but I hoped to out-fumble him. In the third round I cut his eye very badly and shortly after they stopped the fight.

But things were different now in the ring than they had been for me. I could see the punches coming, but I'd move just a fraction too late. Instead of making the other guy miss and banging him, I'd wind up taking the punch myself. And I wasn't built to take punches.

Another thing. When you're young you fight and, in spots, you try to remember to pace yourself. When you're old you pace yourself and, in spots, you try to remember to fight. And the older you get the harder you have to train. Which isn't insurance either, because then you have to worry about going stale.

It was a big change out of the ring, too. A big change from fighting at Madison Square Garden and living at the Ritz. More often than not it was a five dollar a day fleabag with a bathroom down the hall. I only needed the room to sleep the afternoon of the fight from twelve or two until six, so I'd just check in for the day, a day of cracks in the walls and cracks in the bed.

A good buddy of mine, Mike Tominiolo, who I know from the old days when I was champ, got a room once with a double bed with a crack in the middle, so when you laid down the bed would cave in. It's pretty hard to get your proper rest before the fight when the bed caves in. But Mike didn't mind. He is about the only guy who stuck with me over the years. When I was champ everybody was my friend. But when money and fame started to go most of the friends went the same way, except for Mike Tominiolo. Yet, I didn't mind, as long as people around me are happy. Mike said I'm the greatest adjuster in the world. I know I do try to take life as it comes.

Part of the reason I kept fighting was that I had been married and divorced a number of times, and each time I settled outright with these girls. Every time I got divorced I got emptied out, too.

Those girls got everything, but one divorce I remember particularly. About a year before it I was walking along trying to figure out what I'd get my wife for her birthday. As I was walking past this pet shop somebody whistled at me. I turned around, but I didn't see anyone, except this Myna bird caged on the outside. He said, "Hello George." I thought it was kind of cute, so I bought it for my wife. Well, by the time of our divorce all the bird would say was "You're late again, Willie." My wife took everything except the bird. Well, I couldn't have a bird around who never said anything except "You're late again, Willie," so I gave him to my mother and dad. Pretty soon he forgot about my being late and spoke nothing but broken Italian. That was one "bird" I'll never forget.

But it wasn't just the girls. I'd invested in places like Belmont and Aquaduct, too. When you have more money than you need you just become a little careless. You don't see the day when it will stop coming in. But the tracks don't give you any annuities.

So I came back. It was after my fourth divorce, and I was broke. I needed the money. I could make maybe $10,000 or $12,000 a year not boxing. But I liked to box, and I was good at it, and where else could I make $40,00 or $50,000 a year. So I came back. When I was champ I would go out a lot to clubs even when I was training; I never drank or smoked so it didn't hurt when I was young. But it was expensive. I'd drop a thousand dollars in a night gambling. Well, I wasn't champ anymore but I figured I could live like one if I came back. I'd get $1500, maybe $2000 for a fight that was almost like an exhibition. A couple of them a month and I'd be in good shape. I didn't want to quit because I didn't want to do anything else. It, of course, didn't work out that way, but I did fight eleven times in 1965 and won them all.

After my one fight in 1966, I quit. I was called to fight an exhibition in Richmond, Virginia. Fellow said, "Willie, come down and fight this exhibition. You'll get $1000 and all expenses paid." I said, 'Great." So I went down and for three days down there I ate good and stayed at their best hotel.

The day of the fight we went to get weighed in and the commissioner, Bill Brennan, was there. I got on the scales and I weighed 135 pounds. Then Calvin Woodland, a darn good lightweight, got on the scale "Gee, I said, "it's going to feel good to fight an exhibition." But Brennan said to me, "Willie, this is a fight. You're fighting six rounds tonight." I told him that the guy who contacted me, Sam, said this would be an exhibition, not a fight. Then Brennan said to me, "Willie, if you don't fight tonight, you won't get any money, and I'll also blackball you with the World Boxing Association." At the time I was doing a lot of refereeing for the World Boxing Association and I respected them. I was out of shape, but I boxed. I hadn't had a glove on in six months. I don't know if I could have licked him if I were in shape. I was forty-five years old. I boxed him the six rounds and he won the decision. Brennan had told Calvin that if he held back he would hold back his money. So he punched me for six rounds and I had all I could do to hang in there.

Can you imagine a forty-five-year-old guy being punched for six rounds by a twenty-one-year-old kid? I was lucky to get out of there with my scalp on. Yes, this guy Sam had sold me a bill of goods. "Sam the Mumbler," we called him. He had a partner named "Snake-Eyes." They were some pair. That was my last fight.

There are some characters who take advantage of boxers. A young and willing kid who loves to fight if he receives the proper guidance and training from his manager and handler can achieve some real success in boxing. Yet, few boxers ever attain any significant measure of success. Most become so called "opponents" which is another word for a "catcher"—of punches, that is. They have courage and can take lots of punishment yet lack everything else that's needed in boxing. Boxing must protect these kids from the start.

The average fighter is in the ring about four or five years. For every guy like Ray Robinson or Jack Dempsey, there are thousands nobody ever heard of; yet they fought. Some took severe beatings fight after fight and had no business continuing. They should have been forced out before they started "walking on their heels."

Yet the most disappointing aspect in boxing is that a pension system, like in baseball or football, doesn't exist. Maybe there should have been a boxing union! But whatever protection there should have been-it's too late for a lot of the "Heroes" and many of them are familiar household names.

But you know, boxers are sort of different. Like the "club fighter," they always seem to get off the deck in their own way without complaints. You can walk along Broadway or in any other fight town in the country in the wee hours of the morning. You'll see a "Hero" holding an audience of avid sports fans reliving his career. That's his pension- a pocketful of memories.

Well, I was almost home before I knew it, back in Hartford where it all began thirty-two years ago. I crossed Silas Dean Highway near the Dunkin' Donut Shop. I was ten minutes from home. Gerri and Melissa would be waiting for me and my sister Frances would be helping Mom make those Italian holiday cakes like "panettone" and Zeppoli." My brother, Nick would be there too with his family. Pop, who started it all for me, would be the only one missing but we'd be thinking about him.

It was eleven-thirty when I pulled into my driveway, Christmas Eve. Wethersfield was lit up like the marquee of old Madison Square Garden- the way it was every Friday Night.

THE END

Manager Irving Cohen and trainer Whitey Bimstein promote future middleweight Champion Rocky Graziano and their stable of Friday Night fighters that included fistic stars like Billy Graham and Freddie Russo.

WILLIE PEP'S BOXING RECORD

1938

Won the Connecticut State Amateur Flyweight Championship.

1939

Won the Connecticut State Amateur Bantamweight Championship.

1940

July	3	– James McGovern, Hartford	W 4
July	25	– Joey Marcus, Hartford Conn.	W 4
Aug.	8	– Joey Wasnick, New Haven	KO 3
Aug.	29	– Tommy Burns, Hartford, Ct.	KO 1
Sept.	5	– Joey Marcus, New Britain	W 6
Sept.	18	– Jack Moore, Hartford	W 6
Oct.	3	– Jimmy Riche, Waterbury	KO 3
Nov.	22	– Carlo Duponde, New Britain	KO 6
Nov.	29	– Frank Topazio, New Britain	KO 5
Dec.	6	– Jim Mutane, New Britain	KO 2

1941

Jan	28	– Augie Almeda, New Haven	KO 6
Feb.	3	– Joe Echevarria, Holyoke, Mass.	W 6
Feb.	10	– Don Lyons, Holyoke, Mass.	KO 2
Feb.	17	– Ruby Garcia, Holyoke, Mass.	W 6
Mar.	3	– Ruby Garcia, Holyoke, Mass.	W 6

Mar.	25	–	Marty Shapiro, Hartford, Conn.	W 6
Mar.	31	–	Joey Gatto, Holyoke, Mass.	KO 2
Apr.	14	–	Henry Vasquez, Holyoke, Mass.	W 6
Apr.	22	–	Mexican Joey Silva, Hartford	W 6
May	6	–	Lou Puglose, Hartford	KO 2
May	12	–	Johnny Cockfield, Holyoke	W 6
June	24	–	Eddie De Angelis, Hartford	KO 3
July	16	–	Jimmy Gilligan, Hartford	W 8
Aug	1	–	Harry Hitlian, Manchester	W 6
Aug.	5	–	Paul Frechette, Hartford	KO 3
Aug.	12	–	Eddie Flores, Thompsonville	KO 1
Sept.	26	–	Jackie Harris, New Haven	KO 1
Oct.	10	–	Carlos Manzana, New Haven	KO 4
Oct.	22	–	Connie Savoie, Hartford	KO 2
Nov.	7	–	Billie Spencer, Los Angeles	W 4
Nov.	24	–	Dave Crawford, Holyoke	W 8
Dec.	12	–	Ruby Garcia, N.Y.C.	W 4

1942

Jan.	8	–	Joey Rivers, Fall River	KO 4
Jan.	16	–	Sammy Parrota, N.Y.C.	W 4
Jan.	27	–	Abie Kaugman, Hartford	W 8
Feb.	10	–	Angelo Callura, Hartford	W 8
Feb.	24	–	Willie Roach, Hartford	W 8
Mar.	18	–	Johnny Compo, New Haven	W 8
Apr.	14	–	Spider Armstrong, Hartford	KO 4
May	4	–	Curley Nichols, New Haven	W 8
May	12	–	Aaron Seltzer, Hartford	W 8
May	26	–	Joey Iannotti, Hartford	W 8
June	23	–	Joey Archibald, Hartford	W 10
July	21	–	Abe Denver, Hartford	W 12
Aug.	1	–	Joey Silva, Waterbury	KO 7
Aug.	10	–	Pedro Hernandez, Hartford	W 10
Aug.	20	–	Nat Litfin, West Haven	W 10
Sept.	1	–	Bobby Ivy, Hartford	KO 10
Sept.	10	–	Frank Franconeri, N.Y.C.	KO 1
Sept.	22	–	Vince Dell'Orto, Hartford	W 10

Oct. 16 – Joey Archibald, Providence .... W 10
Oct. 27 – George Zengaras, Hartford .... W 10
Nov. 20 – Chalky Wright, New York City .... W 15
            (Won world featherweight championship)
Dec. 14 – Joe Aponte Torres, Wash., D.C. .... KO 7
Dec. 21 – Joy Silva, Jacksonville .... KO 9

1943

Jan. 4 – Vince Dell'Orto, New Orleans .... W 10
Jan. 19 – Bill Speary, Hartford .... W 10
Jan. 29 – Allie Stolz, N.Y.C. .... W 10
Feb. 11 – Davey Crawford, Boston .... W 10
Feb. 15 – Bill Speary, Baltimore .... W 10
Mar. 2 – Lou Transparenti, Hartford .... KO 6
Mar. 19 – Sammy Angott, N.Y.C. ....L 10
Mar. 29 – Bobby McIntire, Detroit .... W 10
Apr. 9 – Sal Bartolo, Boston .... W 10
Apr. 19 – Angel Aviles, Tampa .... W 10
June 8 – Sal Bartolo, Boston .... W 15
            (Title fight)
In U.S. Navy after having served in Army.
Honorably discharged – Jan., 1944

1944

Apr. 4 – Leo Francis, Hartford .... W 10
Apr. 20 – Harold Snooks Lacey, New Haven .... W 10
May 1 – Jackie Leamus, Philadelphia .... W 10
May 19 – Frankie Rubino, Chicago .... W 10
May 23 – Joey Bagnato, Buffalo .... KO 2
June 6 – Julie Kogan, Hartford .... W 10
July 7 – Willie Joyce, Chicago .... W 10
July 17 – Manuel Ortiz, Boston .... W 10
Aug. 4 – Lulu Constantino, Waterbury .... W 10
Aug. 29 – Joey Peralta, Springfield .... W 10
Sept. 19 – Charley Cabey Lewis, Hartford .... KO 10
Sept. 29 – Chalky Wright, New York City .... W 15
            (Title bout)

Oct.	25	– Jackie Leamus, Montreal	W 10
Nov.	14	– Charley Cabey Lewis, Hartford	W 10
Nov.	27	– Pedro Hernandez, Washington	W 10
Dec.	5	– Chalky Wright, Cleveland	W 10

1945

Jan.	23	Ralph Wilson, Hartford	W 10
Feb.	5	– Willie Roache, New Haven	W 10
Feb.	19	– Phil Terranova, New York	W 15
		(Title Bout)	
Mar.	14	– Inducted into U.S. Army.	
Oct.	30	– Paulie Jackson, Hartford	W 8
Nov.	5	– Mike Martyk, Buffalo	KO 5
Nov.	26	– Eddie Giosa, Boston	W 10
Dec.	5	– Harold Gibson, Lewiston	W 10
Dec.	13	– Jimmy McAllister, Baltimore	D 10

1946

Jan.	15	– Johnny Virgo, Buffalo	KO 2
Feb.	13	– Jimmy Joyce, Buffalo	W 10
Mar.	1	– Jimmy McAllister, New York City	KO 2
Mar.	26	– Jackie Wilson, Kansas City	W 10
Apr.	8	– Georgie Knox, Providence	KO 1
May	6	– Ernie Petrone, New Haven	W 10
May	13	– Joey Angelo, Providence	W 10
May	22	– Aponte Torres, St. Louis	W 10
May	27	– Sal Bartolo, New York City	KO 12
		(Title Bout)	
June	7	– Harold Gibson, Buffalo	KO 7
July	25	– Jackie Graves, Minneapolis	KO 8
Aug.	26	– Doll Rafferty, Milwaukee	KO 6
Sept.	4	– Walter Kolby, Buffalo	KO 5
Sept.	17	– Lefty LaChance, Hatford	KO 3
Nov.	1	– Paulie Jackson, Minneapolis	W 3
Nov.	15	– Thomas Beato, Waterbury	KO 2
Nov.	27	– Chalky Wright, Milwaukee	KO 3

1947

Jan.	8	–	Severely injured in airplane crash.		
June	17	–	Victor Flores, Hartford	W	10
July	1	–	Joey Fortuna, Albany	KO	5
July	8	–	Leo Lebrun, Norwalk	W	8
July	11	–	Jean Barriere, No. Adams	KO	4
July	15	–	Paulie Jackson, New Bedford	W	10
July	23	–	Humberto Sierra, Hartford	W	10
Aug.	22	–	Jock Leslie, Flint	KO	12
			(Title Bout)		
Oct.	21	–	Jean Barriere, Portland, Me	KO	4
Oct.	27	–	Archie Wilmer, Phila.	W	10
Dec.	22	–	Alvara Estrada, Lewiston	W	10
Dec.	30	–	Lefty LaChance, Manchester	KO	8

1948

Jan.	6	–	Pedro Biesca, Hartford	W	10
Jan.	12	–	Jimmy Mcallister, St Louis	W	10
Jan.	19	–	Joey Angelo, Boston	W	10
Feb.	24	–	Humberto Sierra, Miami	KO	10
			(World Featherweight Title Bout)		
May	7	–	Leroy Willis, Detroit	W	10
May	19	–	Charley (Cabey) Lewis, Milwaukee	W	10
June	17	–	Miguel Acevedo, Minneapolis	W	10
June	25	–	Luther Burgess, Flint	W	10
July	28	–	Young Junior, Utica	KO	1
Aug.	3	–	Ted Davis, Hartford	W	10
Aug.	17	–	Ted Davis, Hartford	W	10
Sep.	2	–	Johnny Dell, Waterbury	KO	8
Sept.	10	–	Paddy DeMarco, N.Y.C.	W	10
Oct.	12	–	Chuck Burton, Jersey City	W	8
Oct.	19	–	John LaRusso, Hartford	W	10
Oct.	29	–	Sandy Saddler, New York	KO by	4
			(Lost World Featherweight Title)		
Dec.	20	–	Hermie Freeman, Boston	W	10

1949

Jan.	17	– Teddy Davis, St. Louis	W	10
Feb.	11	– Sandy Saddler, N.Y.C.	W	15
		(Re–won World Featherweight title)		
Apr.	27	– Ellis Ask, Detroit	Exh.	4
May	25	– Mel Hammond, St. Paul	Exh.	4
June	6	– Luis Ramos, New Haven	W	10
June	14	– Al Pennino, Pittsfield	W	10
June	20	– Johnny LaRusso, Springfield	W	10
July	12	– Jean Mougin, Syracuse	W	10
Sept.	2	– Miguel Acevedo, Chicago	Exh.	4
Sept.	20	– Eddie Compo, Waterbury	KO	7
		(Title bout)		
Dec.	12	– Harold Dade, St. Louis	W	10

1950

Jan.	16	– Charley Riley, St. Louis	KO	5
		(Title bout)		
Feb.	6	– Roy Andrews, Boston	W	10
Feb.	22	– Jimmy Warren, Miami	W	10
Mar.	17	– Ray Famechon, New York	W	15
		(Title bout)		
May	15	– Art Llanos, Hartford	KO	2
June	1	– Terry Young, Milwaukee	W	10
June	26	– Bobby Timpson, Hartford	W	10
July	25	– Bobby Bell, Washington	W	10
Aug.	2	– Proctor Heinold, Scranton	W	10
Sept.	8	– Sandy Saddler, New York	KO by	8
		(Lost Featherweight title)		

1951

Jan.	30	– Tommy Baker, Hartford	KO	4
Feb.	26	– Billy Hogan, Sarasota	KO	2
Mar.	5	– Carlos Chavez, New Orleans	W	10
Mar.	26	-- Pat Iscobucci, Miami	W	10
Apr.	17	– Bobby Ortiz, St. Louis	KO	5

 177

Apr.   27 – Eddie Chavez, San Francisco .... W 10
June   4 – Jesus Campos, Baltimore .... W 10
Sept.   4 – Corky Gonzales, New Orleans .... W 10
Sept. 26 – Sandy Saddler, New York .... KO by 9
                 (For Featherweight Title)

1952

Apr.   29 – Santiago, Gonzales, Tampa .... W 10
May   5 – Kenny Leach, Columbus, GA .... W 10
May   10 – Buddy Baggett, Aiken, S.C. .... KO 5
May   21 – Claude Hammond, Miami Beach .... W 10
June   30 – Tommy Collins, Boston .... KO by 6
Sept.   3 –   Billy Lima, Pensacola .... W 10
Sept. 11 – Bobby Woods, Vancouver .... W 10
Oct.   1 – Armand Savoie, Chicago .... W 10
Oct.   20 – Billy Lima, Jacksonville .... W 10
Nov.   5 – Manny Castro, Miami Beach .... KO 5
Nov.   19 – Fabala Chavez, St. Louis .... W 10
Dec.   5 – Jorge Sanchez, W. Palm Beach .... W 10

1953

Jan.   19 – Billy Lauderdale, Nassau .... W 10
Jan.   27 – Davey Mitchell, Miami Beach .... W 10
Feb.   10 – Jose Alvarez, San Antonio .... W 10
Mar.   31 – Joey Gambino, Tampa .... W 10
Apr.   7 – Noel Paquette, Miami Beach .... W 10
May   13 – Jackie Blair, Dallas .... W 10
June   5 – Pat Marcune, New York .... KO 10
Nov.   21 – Sonny Luciano, Charlotte .... W 10
Dec.   4 – Davey Allen, West Palm Beach .... W 10
Dec.   8 – Billy Lima, Houston .... KO 2
Dec.   15 – Tony Longo, Miami Beach .... W 10

1954

Jan.	19	–	David Seabrooke, Jacksonville	W	10
Feb.	26	–	Lulu Perez, New York	KO by	2
July	24	–	Mike Turcotte, Mobile	W	10
Aug	18	–	Til LeBlanc, Moncton, N.B.	W	10
Nov.	1	–	Mario Colon, Daytona Beach	W	10

1955

Mar.	11	–	Myrel Olmstead, Bennington, Vt	W	10
Mar.	22	–	Charley Titone, Holyoke	W	10
Mar.	30	–	Gil Cadilli, Parks Airforce Base, Calif.	L	10
May	18	–	Gil Cadilli, Detroit	W	10
June	1	–	Joey Cam, Boston	KO	4
June	14	–	Mickey Mars, Miami Beach	KO	7
July	12	–	Hector Rodriguez, Bridgeport	W	10
Sept.	13	–	Jimmy Ithia, Hartford	KO	6
Sept.	2	–	Henry (Pappy) Gault, Holyoke	W	10
Oct.	10	–	Charley Titone, Brockton	W	10
Nov.	29	–	Henry (Pappy) Gault, Tampa	W	10
Dec.	12	–	Leo Carter, Houston	KO	4
Dec.	28	–	Andy Arel, Miami Beach	W	10

1956

Mar.	13	–	Kid Campeche, Tampa	W	10
Mar.	27	–	Buddy Bagget, Beaumont	W	10
Apr.	17	–	Jackie Blair, Hartford	W	10
May	22	–	Manuel Armenteros, San Antonio	KO	7
June	19	–	Russ Tague, Miami Beach	W	10
July	4	–	Hector Bacquettes, Lawton, Okla	KO	4

1957

Apr.	23	–	Cesar Morales, Ft. Lauderdale	W	10
May	10	–	Manny Castro, Florence, S.C.	W	10
July	16	–	Manny Castro, El Paso	W	10
July	23	–	Russ Tague, Houston	W	10

Dec. 17 – Jimmy Connors, Boston .... W 10

1958

Jan.   14 – Tommy Tibbs, Boston ....L 10
Mar. 31 – Prince Johnson, Holyoke .... W 10
Apr.   8 – George Stephany, Bristol .... W 10
Apr. 14 – Cleo Ortiz, Providence .... W 10
Apr. 29 – Jimmy Kelly, Boston .... W 10
May   20 – Bobby Singleton, Boston .... W 10
June 23 – Pat McCoy, New Bedford .... W 10
July   1 – Bobby Soares, Athol .... W 10
July 17 – Bobby Bell, Norwood .... W 10
Aug.   4 – Luis Carmona, Presque Isle .... W 10
Aug.   9 – Jesse Rodriguez, Painesville .... W 10
Aug. 26 – Al Duarte, No. Adams .... W 10
Sept. 20 – Hogan (Kid) Bassey, Boston .... KO by 9

1959

Jan.   26 – Sonny Leon, Caracas ....L 10
           Announced retirement, January 27, 1959
           Decided on a comeback, January 12, 1965

1965

Jan.   28 – Jerry Powers, Miami ....Exh. 4
Mar. 12 – Hal Mckeever, Miami .... W 8
Apr. 26 – Jackie Lennon, Philadelphia .... W 6
May   21 – Johnny Gilmore, Norwalk .... W 6
May   28 – Irish Bob Shaugnessy ....Exh. 4
July 26 – Benny Randell, Quebec .... W 10
Sept. 28 – Johnny Gilmore, Philadelphia .... W 6
Oct.   1 – Willie Little, Johnston .... KO 3
Oct.   4 – Tommy Haden, Providence .... KO 3
Oct. 14 – Sergio Musquiz, Phoenix .... KO 5
Oct. 25 – Ray Coleman .... KO 5

180

1966

Mar.   16   –   Calvin Woodland, Richmond ....L 6

TB	KO	WD	WF	D	LD	LF	KOBY	ND	NC
241	65	164	0	1	5	0	6	0	0

ELECTED TO BOXING HALL OF FAME 1963.

ACKNOWLEDGEMENTS

Special thanks to Henry Duarte of the Accountants Exchange; Nat Loubet; Editor of Ring Magazine; Scoop Gallelo, President of The International Veterans Boxing Association; Stephen B. Acunto, President of The American Association for the Improvement of Boxing, Inc.; Eugene Ferrara of the New York Daily News Photo Library; Jerry Lisker and Bill Gallo of the New York Daily News; John Gallagher.

Bill Bosio
John (Red) Ghent
Paddy Read

And to all the HEROES..........

Robert Sacchi

Robert Sacchi is familiar to many having worked as an actor on stage, screen and television. FRIDAY'S HEROES is a labor of love - as a pal and fan of Willie Pep as well as the fight game.

Bob holds a masters degree from New York University as well as one from the streets of New York to the Halls of Madison Square Garden.

Joey Adams

Joey Adams is an International Comedian, toastmaster and author of over 26 books. The latest is The Speaker's Bible of Humor. He has a daily radio show and has been cited in the Congressional Record as an outstanding entertainer, humanitarian and world traveler. Mr. Adams has been Goodwill Ambassador for three Presidents of the United States and represented President John F. Kennedy in the troubled area of the world.

He is married to NBC Commentator and syndicated columnist Cindy Adams.

CPSIA information can be obtained at www.ICGtesting.com
Printed in the USA
BVOW071538060313

314864BV00001B/6/P